FROMMER'S
WALKING TOURS
ENGLAND'S
FAVORITE CITIES

BY
DAN LEVINE
AND RICHARD JONES

MACMILLAN TRAVEL
U.S.A.

MACMILLAN TRAVEL
A Prentice Hall/Macmillan Company
15 Columbus Circle
New York, NY 10023

ISBN 0-671-88617-7
LC 94-077064

Design by Robert Bull Design
Maps by Ortelius

SPECIAL SALES
Bulk purchases (10 + copies) of Frommer's Travel Guides are available to
corporations at special discounts. The Special Sales Department can produce custom editions to be used as premiums and/or for sales promotion
to suit individual needs. Existing editions can be produced with custom
cover imprints such as corporate logos. For more information write to:
Special Sales, Prentice Hall, 15 Columbus Circle, New York, NY 10023.

Manufactured in the United States of America

CONTENTS

LIST OF MAPS

INVITATION TO THE READERS

In researching this book, we have come across many wonderful sights, pubs, and restaurants, the best of which we have included here. As you explore the cities in this book, please share your experiences, especially if you want to bring to our attention information that has changed since this book was researched. You can address your letters to:

Dan Levine and Richard Jones
Frommer's Walking Tours: England's Favorite Cities
Macmillan Travel
15 Columbus Circle
New York, NY 10023

SAFETY ADVISORY

Whenever you're traveling in an unfamiliar city or country, stay alert. Be aware of your immediate surroundings. Wear a moneybelt and keep a close eye on your possessions. Be particularly careful with cameras, purses, and wallets, all favorite targets of thieves and pickpockets.

Introducing England's Favorite Cities

There is no better way to get to know a city than to stroll along its streets and byways, and many of England's historic cities lend themselves to just such exploration. The cities in this book, all major tourist destinations, are perfect for walkers. You can stroll at your own pace while our walks guide you to important sites, buildings, and attractions, relating anecdotes about important people and cueing you in to significant historical events to make sure that you don't miss anything.

Our first four tours cover Oxbridge—Cambridge and Oxford, England's oldest universities, with their long and distinguished histories. We move on to Bath, a planned city with its perfect 18th-century architecture and ancient Roman baths. Stratford-upon-Avon, perhaps England's most popular tourist excursion, is famous as the birthplace of William Shakespeare, but it's also one of England's best-preserved Elizabethan towns. Chester is a less well-known destination—but that's part of its charm. One of the pleasantest places in England to explore on foot, it is the only English city still surrounded by a complete medieval wall. And York, with its great cathedral, is almost a historical microcosm of England itself.

OXFORD

The town of Oxford supposedly grew up around a priory founded by St. Frideswide in the 8th century; legend has it that she came to Oxford in flight from a suitor who was struck blind as he entered the town in pursuit, and then had his sight restored by her prayers. Oxford may have originated as a settlement outside the priory gates. Its name, originally "Oxen Ford," comes from its location on a ford in the Thames river. The Saxon town was laid out in a regular manner, and enclosed by a wall with four gates. By 1066 it was an important political center and the sixth-largest town in England. A castle was built by the Normans and later garrisoned by both Royalist and Parliamentary troops in the English Civil War, but only a mound and the tower of the castle church survive today.

Oxford's scholastic roots reach back as far as 1090, but the first reference to a chancellor, indicating an organized university, does not appear until 1214. In the 11th century the town had been a center of wool and cloth trades, but while the university grew and flourished, the town's fortunes declined.

The relationship between the town and the university was never an easy one. The local residents resented having to provide for an increasing influx of students and scholars who took from the town's resources but produced nothing themselves. A serious riot in 1209 caused the university to disband; one group of scholars fled to Cambridge to establish another university there. This was the beginning of a series of conflicts with the town in which the university was usually backed both by royalty and by the church. In 1355 a riot erupted, culminating in the death of several students. The town was fined and the university was given control over markets and rents. This ascendency of gown over town lasted until the 19th century.

During the 15th and 16th centuries, scholars such as Erasmus and Sir Thomas More taught at Oxford and saw the introduction of European humanist scholarship and the revival of classical learning. This was also the period of the Reformation, but although Oxford was visited by Protestants from Cambridge, it remained wary of the new religion. In 1555, the new religion's leading proponents, Archbishop Cranmer and bishops Ridley and Latimer, were imprisoned at Oxford. Ridley and Latimer were later burnt at the stake outside Balliol College in Broad Street—the college's doors were singed by the fire.

In the English Civil War, both town and university were loyal supporters of King Charles I. Oxford became the royalist capital, arms were stored in the colleges, and the town was filled with royalist soldiers. Teaching almost stopped at this time. Oxford withstood one

ENGLAND

siege, but fell in 1646; the king fled and the parliamentary forces occupied the town.

Science and mathematics flourished at the colleges in the late 17th century, but during the 18th century scholarship declined. Reform came in the 19th century with the introduction of the modern examination system and the erection of new buildings for science and research. Oxford's new emphasis on professions such as law, medicine, and politics made it an important factor in political and public life as its graduates filled the civil service to govern the Empire.

The railway, arriving in Oxford in 1843, stimulated the growth of the town. In 1913 William Morris, a manufacturer of motorcycles, first produced the highly successful Oxford Morris car. By 1925, 41% of all cars in Britain were made in Oxford. Other industries were attracted to the area, and Oxford became a prosperous manufacturing center for automobiles and related products. Today Oxford is a thriving industrial town as well as home to the University that has dominated it for 700 years.

CAMBRIDGE

Cambridge, too, grew up as a place where a river could be forded. There was a Roman settlement here by A.D. 43, and probably a bridge. The town's medieval name—it was called Grantabrycge (Granta Bridge) in the *Anglo-Saxon Chronicle*—suggests that it was valued for its bridge. It became a prosperous settlement, first under the Danes and then under the Saxons. A small market town, it was an important port and center for the distribution of grain and other goods. Stourbridge Fair, established in the 13th century or earlier, and by the 17th century the largest fair in England, assured the town's continuing prosperity.

A crucial event in the town's development was the arrival of the first scholars from Oxford in 1209, fleeing the riots of that city. Cambridge University was established, yet the scholars found themselves facing some of the same problems that had plagued them in Oxford. Their presence was a drain on the resources of the town, which retaliated by charging high rents and prices. But in 1231 Henry III forbade the university towns to charge what the universities saw as unfair prices. By royal charter, the bailiffs of Cambridge town were required to swear to maintain the privileges of the University. As always, in any conflict between town and gown, royal favor came down on the side of the University, although the students were often unruly. In the 14th century, as the University grew, the town's configuration was forcibly changed: Henry VI, for example, had a whole section of the town demolished to make way for King's College.

As in Oxford, humanistic scholarship and classical learning were introduced in the 16th century, and far-reaching changes in the curriculum were made under the influence of Erasmus, who was in

Cambridge between 1511 and 1514. Unlike Oxford, Cambridge became a center for the new religious views of the Reformation, and Oxford's Protestant martyrs were all Cambridge men.

During the English Civil War, the town gained a brief ascendency over the university, since it was stoutly parliamentarian—its M.P. was Oliver Cromwell himself!—while the university supported the royalist cause.

At the end of the 17th century, with the presence of Isaac Newton, there was much interest in scientific research, and Cambridge gained a reputation for scientific preeminence that is still intact today. Like Oxford, Cambridge suffered a decline in the 18th century and changed and expanded in the 19th; student numbers grew, and its graduates became an important influence in public life.

The town also developed in the 19th century. With the coming of the railroad, Cambridge town was no longer wholly dependent on agriculture, and added new industries. Although the town today cannot be described as an industrial city, it does have many well-known factories that specialize in electronics and scientific instruments.

BATH

In its long history, Bath has experienced two periods of historical importance. The first was the coming of the Romans, who built an elegant spa with baths and temples to take advantage of the ancient spring's curative waters. Its second period was its transformation into a beautiful 18th-century spa catering to elegant society.

Shortly after the Romans conquered England in A.D. 43, they moved west in search of silver-bearing lead. There they encountered the spring, which was dedicated to Sul, the Celtic goddess of healing. Identifying Sul with their own goddess, Minerva, the Romans built a temple to Sul-Minerva adjacent to the spring, as well as extensive baths; the town that grew up around them was called Aquae Sulis. For nearly four centuries these baths were used by the Romans, but apart from the fact that they fell into ruins after the Romans left, and were later built over and lost from sight, we know little of their history.

The area was of religious importance during the Middle Ages. A nunnery was founded here in the 9th century, and a Benedictine abbey in the 10th. The baths were probably overseen by monks and used for healing purposes. During the reign of Henry I in the 12th century, the King's Bath was built, and by the 16th century three baths were in use. In the 17th century, the baths were visited by a number of royals, including the queen of Charles I, Henrietta

Maria, but it was the visit of Princess Anne (later Queen Anne) in 1702 that set the seal of respectability on Bath and ushered in a period during which Bath became a center for fashionable society—and for all who had social pretensions. Reconstructed by architect John Wood and his son John into a city of elegant crescent rows rising up from the natural amphitheater of the Avon River valley, and financed by entrepreneur Ralph Allen, who first bought a quarry and then sold the stone he quarried to the town for construction, Bath's popularity skyrocketed. It was the place to see and be seen, under the leadership of its master of ceremonies, the flamboyant Richard "Beau" Nash, who ensured the peace of the town by abolishing dueling and who encouraged gambling, inventing new games of chance to circumvent the current laws against it.

Today 18th-century Bath is a town of unparalleled architectural beauty. The Roman baths that have been excavated are only a fraction of what remains to be discovered. Much is still hidden under the Abbey churchyard and the streets around it. Bath was heavily bombed in 1942 as part of a Nazi strategy to demolish historic sites, but since that time, the city has been painstakingly restored to its Georgian splendor.

STRATFORD-UPON-AVON

Long before Stratford became famous for its association with England's greatest playwright it was a flourishing market town, the oldest in Warwickshire.

The site has been inhabited since the Bronze Age. Its name, *straet*, refers to the Roman road that once forded the Avon river. By 1400 the weekly market for the whole region was established at Stratford, as well as several annual fairs, one or two of which still survive today—the fair in Rother Street, now held every Friday, was once a cattle fair. The medieval wealth of the town is evidenced by the fraternity that was formed in the 13th century, to which all the prominent people of the town belonged. The Gild of the Holy Cross contributed to the town's welfare by supporting a school and almshouses as well as giving to charity. When religious organizations were abolished during the Reformation, the members of the fraternity persuaded the king to make Stratford a borough and grant it the Gild properties so that these institutions could still be maintained.

Always prosperous, the town increased its wealth when the Avon was made navigable in the mid-16th century and could be used for trade. Brewing was the principal industry, and a brewery still operates here.

In the 18th century, the cult of Shakespeare, initiated by actor

David Garrick's attempt to present a Shakespeare festival, began the present-day prosperity of the town, which is founded on the Shakespeare name. Interest in Shakespeare prompted much of the restoration of the town's Elizabethan architecture as well as the preservation of the properties connected with Shakespeare himself. Some of these went through many vicissitudes, and may be more Victorian than Elizabethan. Shakespeare's own house, New Place, was demolished by an irate owner who had quarreled with the city corporation, and was irritated by the many visitors who came by. Some, like Anne Hathaway's cottage, survived by chance—it was owned by many generations of the same family.

The town today is virtually a living museum. The layout has not changed since medieval times, and the visitor is offered a real impression of what an Elizabethan town might have looked like.

CHESTER

Of all the towns we've chosen, Chester is most off the beaten path. On a sandstone height above the river Dee, it was founded by the Romans in A.D. 79 as a base for their military operations against the Welsh. They chose a site on the banks of the river where sea-going vessels could moor directly under the protective city walls, sheltered by the river's bend.

When the Romans left Britain, Chester was ravaged by the Danes and then rebuilt by the Saxons. One of the last strongholds to fall to William the Conquerer, who made it into a virtually independent state governed by eight earls, Chester was reinvigorated by the Normans. When the last of these earls died, leaving only a daughter as heir, the king took over the city and conferred the earldom on his son. Ever since, Chester has been a property of the eldest son of the reigning monarch.

By the Middle Ages, Chester was the most important of the northern English ports. Its position on the west coast made it a natural trading port for Irish goods, and a flourishing trade ensued. However, this ended in the 15th century when the Dee silted up, making navigation virtually impossible.

During the English Civil War, King Charles I watched from Chester's walls as his army went down in defeat at the battle of Rowton Moor. For 18 months, the Parliamentarians besieged the city; it fell in 1646. After the war, Chester again flourished, and by the 18th century the city was a thriving commercial center.

The modern city of Chester has a medieval aspect, and is still surrounded by its red sandstone wall, which has a walk along the top. Every type of architecture from Norman to Late Perpendicular is found in Chester. Typical of Chester are the picturesque Rows, houses built with projecting second stories, arcade fashion.

YORK

Lying on the confluence of the Ouse and Foss rivers, York still retains part of its medieval walls and two of its gates.

The Romans founded York in A.D. 71 when they established a fortress that they called *Eboracum*. As capital of Lower Britain, Eboracum became one of the foremost Roman cities in England. The town functioned as a military base for Emperor Hadrian, and it was here that Constantine the Great was crowned as emperor—the only emperor to be proclaimed in Britain.

With the departure of the Romans, York fell into decline. Danish voyagers came here in A.D. 867 and built the town into an important trading center and port. The Vikings called the city *Jorvick,* a name that later became York.

After the Norman conquest, William the Conqueror chose York as one of his primary military centers. William built two castles here and established religious foundations, hospitals, chapels, and churches. The next three centuries were "The Golden Age of York," because the city became a favorite of kings and queens. The monarch's occasional presence made York England's second city, after London.

York's most significant landmark is the great cathedral of York Minster, "minster" being the Saxon name for a large church. There were four earlier churches on this site, but the Minster as it now stands was begun in the reign of Henry III, in about 1220, and was not finished until 1472. The glory of the Minster is its stained and painted glass; it has retained more of its medieval glass than any church in England. York is the ecclesiastical center of the north of England, second only to Canterbury.

During the English Civil War, York remained loyal to the sovereign. It was besieged by Parliamentary forces for three months, and its surrender marked the end of the king's authority in the north. In the 18th century, York became an important English social center, and in the 19th, a transportation hub—first for stagecoaches and then for trains.

It has been said that a walk through York is a stroll through English history—which was our aim in all of the tours we have set out for you.

WALKING TOUR 1

Cambridge Part I

Start: Emmanuel College Gatehouse, St. Andrew's Street.
Finish: Emmanuel College Gatehouse, St. Andrew's Street.
Time: 2 hours, not including rest stops.
Best Times: Monday through Friday from 10am to noon, and again from 2 to 4pm, when most of the sites are open.
Worst Times: Lunchtime and weekends, when many college buildings are closed to the public.

In 1209 a group of students and teachers from riot-torn Oxford established themselves in the flourishing little market town of Cambridge. Like all such medieval institutions, Cambridge University was at first only a guild of teachers with the right to award degrees; students enrolled with a master and lived in hostels, paying for their own board and lodging. Peterhouse was the first college to be established, and by 1475 there were 12 colleges affiliated with the university. By this time, students and teachers were both in residence in the colleges, and the university had come to enjoy an international reputation.

Cambridge's colleges are self-governing bodies that are independently responsible for the admission, accommodation, and education of their undergraduates. The university that unites them establishes graduation requirements and administers final exams, a system that has survived from the 15th century to the present day.

Cambridge is arguably one of the most attractive towns in England. The older colleges of Cambridge University are laid out along the river Cam, with its grassy banks and many bridges. Punting on the river is a favorite sport, and students can often be seen propelling the flat boats along by thrusting a long pole against the shallow river bed.

Our two walking tours have been carefully planned to show you as many of the town's colleges as possible.

Start at the main entrance of:

1. **Emmanuel College,** located on St. Andrew's Street, just opposite Downing Street. The school was founded in 1584 on the site of a former Dominican priory by Sir Walter Mildmay, Queen Elizabeth I's chancellor of the exchequer.

    Enter the college through the arched gatehouse, and immediately turn left onto the cobblestone pathway. Walk straight, through the swinging doors, turn right at the kitchens, and continue straight through the doorway at the far corner. Through the window to your right is:

2. **The Old Library,** which was formerly the refectory of the Dominican priory. Unfortunately, the library is closed to the public, but you can view its most important room through the window here.

    Turn left, walk through the swinging doors, and at the end of the passageway turn left again, into the cloistered walkway. A quick jog right and then left takes you to:

3. **Emmanuel Chapel,** which was completed in 1677 according to a design by master architect Sir Christopher Wren. The second stained-glass window on your left depicts John Harvard, an Emmanuel student, and benefactor of the American university that bears his name. Harvard and other religious puritans immigrated to America in the 1630s to escape religious and social intolerance in England.

    After viewing the chapel's most interesting feature—the altar painting called *The Return of the Prodigal*—exit the building, and retrace your steps to the college's gatehouse. Turn right onto St. Andrew's Street, crossing Emmanuel Street and Bradwell's Court, and you will come to:

4. **Christ's College,** situated on your right. Originally called

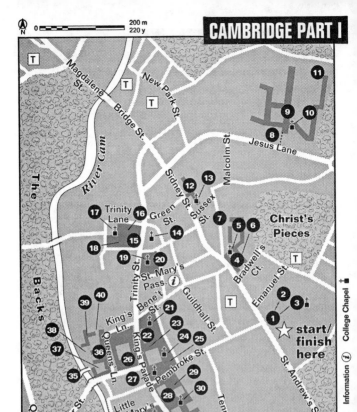

0 — 200 m
0 — 220 y

Magdalene St.
New Park St.
Bridge St.
Jesus Lane
River Cam
The
Sidney St.
Malcolm St.
Green St.
Sussex St.
Trinity Lane
Christ's Pieces
Hobson Street
Bradwell's Ct.
St. Mary's Pass.
Bene't St.
Emanuel St.
Guildhall St.
start/ finish here
King's Ln.
St. Andrew's St.
Queens' Ln.
King's Parade
Pembroke St.
Backs
Trinity St.
Tennis Court Rd.
Silver St.
Little St. Mary's Ln.
Queen's Rd.
St. Granta Pl.
Trumpington St.

Public Toilets [T]   Information *i*   College Chapel

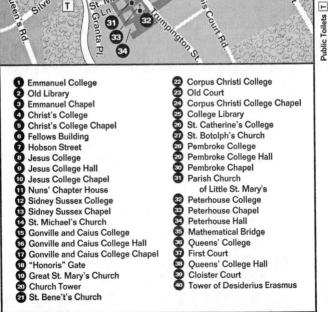

1 Emmanuel College
2 Old Library
3 Emmanuel Chapel
4 Christ's College
5 Christ's College Chapel
6 Fellows Building
7 Hobson Street
8 Jesus College
9 Jesus College Hall
10 Jesus College Chapel
11 Nuns' Chapter House
12 Sidney Sussex College
13 Sidney Sussex Chapel
14 St. Michael's Church
15 Gonville and Caius College
16 Gonville and Caius College Hall
17 Gonville and Caius College Chapel
18 "Honoris" Gate
19 Great St. Mary's Church
20 Church Tower
21 St. Bene't's Church

22 Corpus Christi College
23 Old Court
24 Corpus Christi College Chapel
25 College Library
26 St. Catherine's College
27 St. Botolph's Church
28 Pembroke College
29 Pembroke College Hall
30 Pembroke Chapel
31 Parish Church
   of Little St. Mary's
32 Peterhouse College
33 Peterhouse Chapel
34 Peterhouse Hall
35 Mathematical Bridge
36 Queens' College
37 First Court
38 Queens' College Hall
39 Cloister Court
40 Tower of Desiderius Erasmus

6663

"God's House," and located on nearby Milne Street, Christ's College was granted its Royal Charter on May 1, 1505, at the behest of Bishop John Fisher, confessor to King Henry VII's mother, Lady Margaret Beaufort. Above the college's gatehouse is a statue of Lady Margaret, along with her coat of arms supported by mythical beasts called "Yales." Lady Margaret frequently came to stay at the college, and no doubt saw to it that her rules were observed: The college gates were to be locked at 9pm in winter and 11pm in summer, and only Latin was to be spoken in college; students were forbidden to take part in drinking parties, carry weapons, keep dogs or hawks, or play with dice or cards.

Walk through the gatehouse into the college's first courtyard. A small passageway on your left leads to rooms that were once occupied by the poet John Milton (1608–1674). This author of *Paradise Lost,* and other seminal works of English literature, studied and taught here from 1625 to 1632. Milton was not popular, and was known to his fellow students as "The Lady of Christ's" because of his delicate appearance. Charles Darwin was also a student here.

At the far left corner of the courtyard, almost hidden among the bushes, is the entrance to:

5. **Christ's College Chapel,** a 15th-century building that was enlarged in 1506. Entering the main body of the chapel, you immediately encounter the chapel's spectacular Eagle Lectern, regarded by scholars as one of the finest pre-Reformation reading desks in England. To your right is Lady Margaret's Window, so called because it allowed King Henry VII's mother to look inside the chapel from her private rooms in the adjacent lodge. In the left-hand corner of the stained-glass window above the altar, Lady Margaret is portrayed with her confessor, Bishop Fisher. In the right-hand corner is a depiction of Henry VII, and at the center, above them all, stands Christ on a purple cloud.

The monument to the left of the altar is an interesting dual memorial to two close friends who were both fellows, Professor Sir Thomas Baines and Sir John Finch, physician. The two became friends during their student days and remained practically inseparable for the rest of their lives. When Baines died in Constantinople, Finch had his friend's body embalmed and sent to Christ's College for burial. Finch himself died just a few months later and was buried beside his friend.

Exit the chapel, and turn left across the chapel porch into the next court. The building directly in front of you is the:

6. **Fellows Building,** a college dormitory, built from 1640 to

1643 by an unknown architect. The wrought-iron gates in the center of the building lead to The Fellows' Garden, which was laid out in the early 19th century with a small bathing pool and a bust of poet John Milton. Popular legend holds that the adjacent mulberry tree was planted by the great poet himself, though it is more likely that the tree is one of 300 that were planted by the college in 1608, the year of Milton's birth. The garden is open Monday through Friday from 10:30am to 12:30pm, and again from 2 to 4pm.

Retrace your footsteps to the gatehouse, exit the college and turn right onto St. Andrew's Street. The next intersection is:

7. **Hobson Street,** named for Thomas Hobson (1544–1631), a mail carrier and stable owner who is said to have balked at tradition by not allowing his customers the horse of their choice; he always insisted they take the horse nearest the door. He was made famous by Milton's humorous epitaphs on his death. Thus began the expression "Hobson's Choice," a term that refers to a situation in which there appear to be no alternatives.

Turn right onto Hobson Street, bear right at the telephone boxes, then turn left onto Malcolm Street. After one long block, turn right onto Jesus Lane, then left through the gatehouse, onto the bicycle-lined pathway known as "The Chimney." This path leads into:

8. **Jesus College.** In 1496, John Alcock, Bishop of Ely visited the 12th-century Benedictine nunnery of St. Radegund that once stood here, and was horrified to find it in a ruinous and impoverished state, occupied by only two remaining nuns. The bishop petitioned King Henry VII and obtained a license to close the nunnery, establishing in its place "The College of the Blessed Virgin Mary, St. John the Evangelist and the Glorious Virgin St. Radegund," which quickly became known more simply as Jesus College. The following year, Alcock built the school's magnificent gatehouse tower and surmounted it with a statue of himself.

Turn right onto the pathway, and walk to the archway. Just inside the archway, turn left through the wooden doors and walk up the stairs to:

9. **Jesus College Hall.** Originally built as the nuns' refectory, the hall has been in continuous use as a dining chamber for over 800 years. The room features a beautiful three-sided oriel, or bay, window, antique paneling around the dais that dates from 1703, and an early 16th-century timbered roof. The portrait at the far end of the hall is of Henry VIII.

Exit Jesus College Hall, return downstairs to the passageway, and continue along the path that jogs left, then right, into a

16th-century cloistered court. Follow the cloisters around to the left, then turn right, into:

10. Jesus College Chapel, the oldest building in any Cambridge college. Originally part of the nuns' church, the chapel's choir dates from the 13th century. The stained-glass windows, by pre-Raphaelite painter Edmund Burne-Jones and the colorful ceiling by William Morris were added in a 19th-century restoration. Turn left up the aisle, then right, into the south transept where, on your left, there is a memorial to Jesus student and poet Samuel Taylor Coleridge (1772–1834). The inscription on the memorial is a verse from one of Coleridge's best known works, *The Rime of the Ancient Mariner:*

> *He prayeth best who loveth best*
> *all things both great and small*
> *for the dear God who loveth us*
> *he make and loveth all.*

Coleridge had an uneventful graduate career, and abandoned college to join the British army under the assumed name Silas Tomkins Comerbacke. Finding the army even less desirable than school, the poet soon returned to Cambridge. However, Coleridge shortly found himself both in debt and at ideological odds with the college faculty, prompting him to leave Cambridge once again. Despite all this, Coleridge would later in his life often look back at his Cambridge days with fondness and recall the "friendly cloisters and happy grove of quiet, ever honoured Jesus College."

On the wall to the right of the Coleridge memorial is yet another homage to a Jesus fellow; this one dedicated to Archbishop Thomas Cranmer (1489–1556). While a student, Cranmer married, and since this was forbidden by college rules, he was promptly expelled, only to be reinstated a short time later after his wife died in childbirth. Cranmer went on to become the first Protestant archbishop of Canterbury and was later burned in Oxford during Mary Tudor's reign for his adherence to the Protestant faith.

Exit the chapel, turn right, and follow the cloisters all the way around to the remains of the entrance to the:

11. Nuns' Chapter House, which was destroyed by Jesus College founder Bishop Alcock. The arches that remain date from about 1230, and were hidden until 1893, when a keen-eyed fellow discovered them under a thick coat of plaster.

Continue walking around the cloisters, and exit the college.

Turn right onto Jesus Lane, walk two long blocks, turn left onto Sidney Street and continue one block. On your left will be:

12. Sidney Sussex College. Founded in 1594, the college was built with money bequeathed by Lady Frances Sidney, the Countess of Sussex. As Lady Frances had no children, her will poetically stipulated that "such learned persons who receive their breeding in her Foundation may be termed her issue."

Enter the college gates, turn right, pass through the archway, turn left, and at the end of the path turn right, where, on the left, is the entrance to:

13. Sidney Sussex Chapel. Actually, the first room you enter is the antechapel, where the plaque set just to the left of the main door is worth noting. The plaque commemorates Oliver Cromwell (1599–1658), England's 17th-century Lord Protector, leader of the Parliamentarian forces in the English Civil War. Upon his death in 1658, Cromwell was buried in Westminster Abbey, England's most illustrious burial place. Two years later, however, the monarchy was restored and Cromwell's body was exhumed, hanged, and beheaded. Cromwell's head was skewered on a spike and positioned high above London's Westminster Hall where it remained for 20 years, before blowing down in a gale. The head was recovered by a night watchman who took it home as a family memento. For the next 300 years Cromwell's head passed to various owners, until Dr. H. N. S. Wilkinson brought it here in 1960. In order to protect the head from would-be Royalist thieves, it was buried in a secret location close to this spot. The plaque in front of you reads "Near to this place was buried on 25th March, 1960 the head of Oliver Cromwell, Lord Protector of the Commonwealth of England, Scotland, and Ireland. Fellow commoner of this college 1616–17."

Enter the main body of the chapel which was built in 1782, then regularly altered and added-to every few decades, until 1923. Today, the church is considered a fine example of modern ecclesiastical architecture in the neobaroque style. The chapel's intricately carved oak stalls and paneling are particularly worth close inspection. The altar painting, depicting the holy family, is the work of Giovanni Battista Pittoni (1687–1767), and the statue to the right of the altar is of St. Francis.

Exit the chapel, turn right, and walk into the passageway and through the courtyard. To the left of the bushes is another small passageway that opens into a cloistered courtyard. After exploring the school's grounds, return to the main gates, exit the college, turning left onto Sidney Street, then right onto Green Street to:

REFUELING STOP W. Eaden Lilley and Co. Ltd., Green Street (tel. 0223/35 8822). Inside this large Cambridge department store is a low-cost café that's popular with students and locals. Dining is at a couple of small tables, and on bar stools fronting the windows. Sandwiches, fish and chips, shepherd's pie, and other English specialties are served. The café is open Monday through Saturday from 11am to 4pm.

Continue to the end of Green Street and turn left onto Trinity Street where one block ahead on your left is:

14. St. Michael's Church. Although this isn't the highlight of your Cambridge tour, the church, which was built before A.D. 1200 and redesigned in 1326, is worth a peek inside. Although St. Michael's is not a college-owned church, the design of its oversized nave was the prototype for most of Cambridge's college chapels.

A few steps farther along Trinity Street, opposite the church, is:

15. Gonville and Caius College, named for its 1348 founder Edmund Gonville, and 1558 patron John Kaye, known by his Latin name, *Caius* (both pronounced *Keys*). Caius graduated from Gonville in 1529, studied medicine in Italy at the University of Padua, and returned to England to serve as royal physician to Edward VI, Mary Tudor, and Elizabeth I. Caius is also credited with introducing the study of practical anatomy to England. In 1557 Caius obtained a royal charter to refound his alma mater as Gonville and Caius College, and it was rededicated a year later. Caius then appointed himself the school's master and, although he accepted no payment for the position, insisted on some very peculiar rules of admission including a stipulation that the college bar entry to those who were "deaf, dumb, lame, chronic invalids, or Welshmen."

Caius had three symbolic entrance gates built, each one representing a stage in a student's college life. Walking through the first one, notice the word *Humilitatis,* Latin for "humility," emblazoned across its top. The student entered through this small gate to begin his academic career, passed through the beautiful gate of "Virtue" (which you see just opposite as you enter the college), and finally, when he was worthy, walked through the gate of "Honor."

Once through the first gate, turn right and walk to the end of the pathway to the statue of Caius. Turn left at the statue, walk to the end of the path, descend the steps, and continue through the tunnel into the next courtyard. Just ahead is:

16. Gonville and Caius College Hall, the college's primary dining and meeting hall. Several curious artifacts inside include a portrait of William Harvey, who is credited with the discovery of blood circulation; and a small flag, the college standard, which was flown at the South Pole by explorer Dr. Edward A. Wilson, a member of Captain Robert Scott's 1912 Antarctic expedition. The hall is open Monday through Friday from 10am to noon, and again from 2:30 to 6pm.

Exit the hall, turn left, and walk under the archway to:

17. Gonville and Caius College Chapel, which is located on your left. The chapel's interior, which dates from 1637 is particularly beautiful and definitely worth more than a glance. Look up at the molded representation of sun rays and cherubs on the ceiling.

Exit the chapel, turn left through the archway, and walk straight across the pathway to the splendid:

18. "Honoris" Gate, one of the most-photographed monuments in Cambridge. Its novel design, which incorporates six sundials, is said to have been inspired by an ancient Roman-era tomb.

Exit the college through this gate and turn left, onto the pathway known as Senate House Passage. Beware of the student cyclists who cruise this corridor at breakneck speed. At the end of the path, turn right onto Trinity Street. One block ahead on your left is:

19. Great St. Mary's Church. There has been a church on this site since the 11th century, and the current structure dates from 1478. Great St. Mary's has long been associated with the colleges of Cambridge, hosting both religious and secular university-related functions. Despite its close ties to academia, the church was never incorporated into a particular Cambridge school, and has remained instead a parish church. Nicholas Ridley, Hugh Latimer, and Thomas Cranmer, the Protestant martyrs burned at Oxford (see Stops 5 and 13 in "Walking Tour 4"), all preached regularly in this church.

The church's entrance is around the corner; turn left onto St. Mary's Passage and, before entering, notice:

20. The Church Tower, begun in 1491, completed in 1536, modified in 1593, and equipped with bells in 1793. The last addition, the clock's chimes, makes this tower special. The chimes' melody, composed by two Cambridge undergraduates named Crotch and Pratt, became famous after it was copied for the "Big Ben" clock tower of London's Houses of Parliament. The tune is said to have been inspired by the aria from Handel's oratorio, *Messiah*, "I know that my redeemer liveth." Thus, the tune known throughout the world as the Westminster Chimes is in fact the Cambridge Chimes.

While the church's relatively plain interior is not as colorful as the building's history, it is definitely worth a look. If you have the stamina, it's also worth climbing the 123 steps to the top of the church's tower, where you will be treated to some fine views over Cambridge. There is a small admission charge.

Exit the church, turning right, onto St. Mary's Passage, then turn left onto Trinity Street, which soon changes its name to King's Parade. Walk about five short blocks, turn left onto Bene't Street, then immediately right into:

21. St. Bene't's Church. The church's Saxon Tower has the distinction of being the oldest surviving building in Cambridge; it dates from 1025. The church's interior is not particularly remarkable, but it contains a few unusual artifacts worth noting. One of these is a long pole with a hook on the end, that's located just behind the baptismal font. This is a 17th-century fire hook, left here as a reminder of the days when these devices were used to drag burning thatch off buildings' roofs. Thomas Hobson (see Stop 7, above) is the most famous of the many people buried in this church.

Exit the church, and cross Bene't Street, into:

REFUELING STOP The Eagle, Bene't Street (tel. 0223/301286).The Eagle pub is best-known for its ceiling, which is branded with the names of British and American airmen. One night in 1940, a young man suddenly placed a chair on a table, climbed onto it with his cigarette lighter in hand, and made the first shaky, sooty inscription on the bar's ceiling. Thus began a historical record which was continued throughout World War II by men of the RAF (Royal Air Force) and the AAF (American Air Force).

Excellent pub food usually means a varied menu of shepherd's pie, steak and kidney pie, and other hot lunches.

Exit the pub, cross Bene't Street, and walk through the iron gates that are located just to the right of St. Bene't's Church. The wooden doorway in front of you is the side entrance to:

22. Corpus Christi College, which was established in 1352, and was originally known as Bene't College. Alone among the colleges of Cambridge, Corpus Christi was founded not by clergy or noblemen, but by townspeople, most of whom were members of the religious guilds of Corpus Christi and of the Blessed Virgin Mary.

Turn left through the entrance where a brown, wall-mounted memorial commemorates Corpus Christi fellow and playwright Christopher Marlowe (1564–1593), perhaps Shakespeare's only poetic rival. Marlowe began school here in 1578 and stayed for almost 10 years. He was killed in a tavern brawl in 1593, the same year that playwright John Fletcher (1579–1625), who is also commemorated on this wall, arrived at Corpus Christi College.

Just past the memorial wall is the:

23. Old Court, Cambridge's first enclosed quadrangle, completed in 1378. The quad has hardly changed in over 600 years. Constructed as student dormitories, the buildings surrounding the Old Court were intended to house four students per room, were not heated, and had floor coverings made of reeds. The windows, which are original, have recessed jams and oversized sills that were designed to hold the oiled linens which were used to keep cold out before glass was installed. Continue walking on the pathway which curves left. Halfway down the path, turn right, through the archway, and climb the four stairs. Straight ahead on your left is the entrance to:

24. Corpus Christi College Chapel, a relatively ordinary structure of restrained design that, with the exception of some fine 16th-century stained glass, is not particularly noteworthy. More significant is:

25. The College Library, located adjacent to the chapel. The library's chief treasure is a vast collection of manuscripts, many of them from the monasteries dissolved by Henry VIII in 1538 to 1539, that once belonged to 16th-century Cambridge master Archbishop Matthew Parker. The most valuable works include a 6th-century Canterbury Gospel believed to have been given to St. Augustine by Pope Gregory the Great, and three dozen Anglo Saxon manuscripts from A.D. 1000, including *The Anglo-Saxon Chronicle,* one of the most important documents of the period. His valuable gift notwithstanding, Archbishop Parker is best remembered for interfering in other people's affairs, a penchant which earned him the lasting nickname "Nosey Parker."

Take note of the portrait in the hall of the library. Discovered in the building's attic earlier this century, the painting, dated 1585, depicts an unnamed young man and the words "this was him in the 21st year of his age." This cryptic evidence has led experts to presume that the portrait is of Christopher Marlowe, who was 21 years old in 1585. The library is usually open Monday through Friday from 2 to 4pm.

Exit the chapel, turn right, and exit the college through the gatehouse in front of you. Cross King's Parade and walk straight, through the brown door across the street. Once through the door, turn right, into the main courtyard of:

26. St. Catherine's College. Founded in 1473, the college was established for a small society of priests intent on studying theology exclusively. In fact, the study of secular subjects, such as medicine and law, was expressly forbidden. Economic pressures in the 16th century eventually induced St. Catherine's to alter its charter, and the curriculum was opened to nonecclesiastical courses.

The college claims among its alumni one of Cambridge's youngest graduates, a 19th-century fellow named William Wotton. It is said that by the time he was 6, this prodigy spoke Latin, Greek, and Hebrew. Wotton "came up" to Cambridge at age 9. Like so many other gifted children, however, Wotton's adult years proved relatively uneventful.

Exit St. Catherine's College, turn right, onto King's Parade, and walk one block to:

27. St. Botolph's Church, a parish church that has been in continuous use since 1320. The current structure stands on the Saxon foundations of Trumpington Gate, one of the entrances in the protective stone wall that once surrounded Cambridge. Fittingly, St. Botolph is the patron saint of travelers.

Enter the church, where, just inside on your right, is the royal coat of arms of King William IV. Ahead, on your left, is a baptismal font covered by an intricately carved canopy, which dates from 1636.

Exit the church and turn left onto King's Parade, which at this point is actually called Trumpington Street. A half-block past Pembroke Street, turn left through the gatehouse of:

28. Pembroke College. Founded in 1347 as The Hall of Marie Valence, the college was begun by Marie St. Pol de Valence, the French-born countess of Pembroke. Marie was only 17 years old when she married the 50-year-old earl of Pembroke. According to legend, Marie's husband died on their wedding day, during a supposedly cordial joust with a friend. This casualty of merriment may have influenced the college's charter, which stipulates that faculty and students must report to authorities if their companions drink too much, quarrel, are extravagant, or visit disorderly houses.

The gatehouse through which you are passing is the oldest in Cambridge. Continue walking straight, into:

29. Pembroke College Hall, the college's main eating and meeting place. The hall was destroyed and rebuilt in the 19th century after one of the fellows, Alfred Waterhouse, convinced his colleagues that the old one was structurally unsafe and in danger of imminent collapse. Waterhouse was proved wrong, however, as several barrels of gunpowder were required to demolish it.

Exit the hall, turn left, then right, toward the arched cloisters. At the cloisters, turn left into:

30. Pembroke Chapel, Sir Christopher Wren's first architectural work, and one of the first English churches to be built in the classical style (preceded only by Inigo Jones's St. Paul's Church in London's Covent Garden).

Today, chapels in the colleges are commonplace, but Pembroke College was the first in Cambridge to have a chapel of its own. Before the advent of college chapels, students and faculty members worshipped in nearby parish churches. Soon after Pembroke's charter was granted, Marie Valence obtained a special bull from the Pope granting her the right to build a private chapel for the college. The original chapel was constructed at the northwest corner of the college. The current structure was financed by Matthew Wren (1565–1667), a Pembroke fellow and bishop of Ely, who entrusted the building's design to his nephew, Christopher Wren, then a professor of astronomy at Oxford. Dedicated on St. Matthew's Day (Sept. 21, 1665), the church was designed with a burial vault that would become Matthew Wren's final resting place two years later. Upon his death, the bishop bequeathed the college a share of the furniture from his private palace chapel at Ely, including the altar plate and the remarkable stall cushions that bear his coat of arms.

To the right of the altar is Ridley's Chair, a seat that was used by bishop, church reformer, and Pembroke fellow Nicholas Ridley (1500–1555). One of the editors of the Book of Common Prayer, Ridley was accused of heresy and burned at the stake (see Stops 5 and 13 in "Walking Tour 4"). Shortly before he was put to death, Ridley wrote a moving letter of farewell in which he waxed lyrical about his time at Pembroke. "Farewell therefore Cambridge, my loving mother and tender nurse. . . . Farewell

Pembroke Hall, of late mine own college, my care and my charge . . . in thy orchard . . . I learned without book almost all Paul's Epistles . . . the sweet smell thereof I trust I shall carry with me into heaven. . . ."

The chapel was originally designed to accommodate about 80 worshipers. In 1880 architect George Gilbert Scott was called in to increase the building's size, moving Wren's east wall about 20 feet to provide for a new sanctuary.

Exit the chapel and retrace your footsteps to the college's main gate. Turn left onto Trumpington Street, then right, onto Little St. Mary's Lane, where a half block ahead on your left is the entrance to:

31. **The Parish Church of Little St. Mary's,** also known as Our Lady of Grace, dedicated November 3, 1354 by the bishop of Ely. Inside the church, above the table that's just to the left of the door, is a memorial to Godfrey Washington, a great uncle of U.S. President George Washington. The plaque reads, "Near this place lyeth the body of the late Rev. Mr. Godfrey Washington of the County of York. Minister of this church and Fellow of St. Peter's College. Born July 26th 1670 and died 28th day of September 1729." The memorial also includes the Washington family's coat of arms—stars and stripes and an eagle—similar to the emblem of the city of Washington, D.C., and said to have influenced the design of the U.S. flag.

Exit the church, return to Trumpington Street and turn right. Walk one block and turn right, into the gates of:

32. **Peterhouse,** the oldest college in Cambridge, founded in 1284 by Hugh de Balsham, Bishop of Ely. Poet Thomas Gray, author of "Elegy Written in a Country Church Yard," was enrolled here from 1742 to 1756. The poet didn't get along well with the other students, whom he routinely characterized as drunkards. Believing his dorm room to be a fire hazard, Gray had an iron bar fitted outside his window, to which he attached a rope ladder for emergency escapes. Gray was so disturbed by the teasing of his fellow students, who stood under his window and shouted "Fire!" that he eventually transferred to Pembroke College.

Walk through the college gates' three arches, continue down the ramp, and turn right. Almost immediately on your right is:

33. **Peterhouse Chapel,** an architecturally interesting building in that it reflects the artistic transition from Gothic to Renaissance styles that took place under the Stuarts. Built in 1628, the building was seriously damaged by Cromwell's anti-Royalist forces in the 1650s. Acting with commendable foresight, church officials removed many of the building's most valuable artifacts

before Cromwell's Parliamentarians arrived. So although much of the church's original stained glass was destroyed, the spectacular east window, which was hidden away, survives intact. Replaced after the restoration of the monarchy in 1660, the window depicts the crucifixion, and is based on Rubens' *Le Coup de Lance*. The church's beautiful ceiling, sparkling with gilded depictions of suns, is also worth noting.

Exit the chapel and cross diagonally left over the cobblestones. Halfway along, turn left through the wooden door. Just inside, on your left, is:

34. Peterhouse Hall, the college's social headquarters, constructed in 1268, and restored in the 1860s. Almost all the Hall's frills, from wall decorations to fireplace tiles to the glass of the oriel, or bay, window, were designed by William Morris, a pre-Raphaelite, who was one of England's most famous interior designers.

Exit the hall, turn left, continue down the passage, and walk through the wooden door at the other end to admire the gardens before backtracking to the college's main gate. Exit Peterhouse, turn left onto Trumpington Street, and turn left into Mill Lane. Two blocks ahead, on your left, is:

REFUELING STOP The Mill Public House, Mill Lane (tel. 0223/357026). Located at the end of Mill Lane, on the banks of the River Cam, The Mill Pub is a favorite student hang-out. Ploughman's lunches and rotating hot dishes are served daily.

Exit The Mill onto Laundress Lane, the small alleyway that begins just opposite. To keep the lane quiet, a sign on your right, dated March 25th, 1857, orders "No throughfare for carriages or horses. . . ." At the end of Laundress Lane turn left, onto Silver Street, and pause in the middle of the bridge. Look to your right, at:

35. Mathematical Bridge, named for its clever 18th-century construction, supposedly accomplished without screws or nails. In 1902, students disassembled the bridge to learn how the feat was achieved, then were unable to reconstruct it. Many people believe that the bridge's fastenerless construction is a myth. In any event, the bridge now stands only with the help of nuts and bolts.

Retrace your footsteps down Silver Street and turn left onto Queen's Lane. About a half block ahead on your left is:

36. Queens' College, founded as St. Bernard's College in 1446. The institution's name changed in 1448, when Queen Margaret of Anjou was granted permission by her husband, Henry VI, to re-found the college and rename it "The Queen's College of St. Margaret and St. Bernard." After Edward IV won the throne from Henry VI in the Wars of the Roses, his wife, Elizabeth Woodville, became Queen's College's patroness in 1465 and the apostrophe in the college's name moved to commemorate both queens.

Enter the college gates into the:

37. First Court, a yard that hasn't changed much since it was originally constructed, back in 1449. The court's durable red bricks were probably imported from Holland, and the sundial, to your right, which dates from 1773, is one of the finest of its kind in Britain.

Walk down the steps and turn right, through the passageway known as "The Screens," and enter:

38. Queens' College Hall, a marvelous 16th-century dining and meeting room. Under a particularly colorful ceiling are portraits of the Dutch humanist Erasmus, Elizabeth Woodville, and Sir Thomas Smith, secretary of state under Queen Elizabeth I. The tiles above the magnificent fireplace depict the months of the year, and are the work of the interior design firm of William Morris.

Exit the hall, turn right, descend the three steps and turn right again, into:

39. Cloister Court. The timber-framed building across the court is the President's Lodge, and dates from about 1597. It is the only one of its kind in Cambridge—all the others burned down long ago.

Walk towards the lodge, turn left down the central pathway, then right, into the cloisters. Follow them as they bear around to the right. Stopping by the wooden recess halfway down on your right, look across the courtyard at:

40. The Tower. Desiderius Erasmus, one of Europe's most famous humanists, and a scholar and writer, lived here. Erasmus (1466–1536) was Queens' College Professor of Divinity from 1511 to 1514, and introduced humanist scholarship to Cambridge. Erasmus was equally unimpressed with the high costs and cold climate of Cambridge, calling it "raw, small, and windy." The college ale excited him even less. However, he did find a few bright spots. Erasmus later referred to Cambridge's women as "the kissing kind," and he looked back with affection on the university's hospitality.

Retrace your footsteps to the college entrance. Exit the main gate, turn right onto Queens' Lane, then left onto Silver Street. You can return to this tour's starting point by turning right, onto King's Parade, then left, onto Pembroke Street, which becomes Downing Street and ends at the Emmanuel College Gatehouse.

Cambridge Part II

Start: King's College, King's Parade.
Finish: Magdalene College, Magdalene Street.
Time: 1½ hours, not including rest stops.
Best Times: Monday through Friday from 10am to noon, and again from 2 to 4pm, when most of the sites are open.
Worst Times: Lunchtime and weekends, when many colleges buildings are closed to the public.

Cambridge competes with Oxford in everything. It loses in age—and usually in boat races—but it wins on charm. The magnificent town is dotted with spires and turrets, as well as drooping willows and daffodils. The romantically named Bridge of Sighs is the centerpiece of St. John's College, which itself is located in a town center that is devoid of cars. Most of the college buildings are clustered near here, and it is their stunning architecture that makes Cambridge worth a visit.

Start at the main entrance of:
   1. King's College, located on King's Parade, right in the geographical center of Cambridge. The school was founded in 1441

by King Henry VI expressly for the purpose of further educating the graduates of the King's other school, Eton School, in Berkshire. Henry's grandiose architectural scheme for the college was only just beginning to take shape when it was interrupted by the outbreak of the Wars of the Roses in 1455. Six years later King Henry was deposed and later died in the Tower of London.

In 1485 Henry Tudor defeated Richard III at the battle of Bosworth and began, as Henry VII, consolidating his new kingdom. Arriving in Cambridge with his mother Lady Margaret Beaufort in 1506, the king pledged himself to the completion of several pious enterprises that Henry VI had begun, including King's College Chapel. The rest of the college's buildings—many constructed according to King Henry VI's original plan—weren't completed until 1730.

Enter the college through the gatehouse. The building directly ahead of you is the:

2. Fellows Building. Built of white Portland stone, this structure is considered by many to be the finest work of noted builder and architect James Gibbs.

Turn right and walk along the pathway. Don't stray from the path, since only the fellows are allowed to walk on the grass. Until 1882, college fellows were forbidden to marry and so they were given special privileges such as this to compensate them.

The pathway leads you to:

3. King's College Chapel. Before entering the building, notice the huge exterior buttresses that support it. As you can see from the different colors of the stones used in construction, the chapel was built in three distinct stages, between 1441 and 1506. Enter the chapel and turn right. Its difficult not to be impressed by the building's delicate fan-vaulted roof. Directly ahead of you is the chapel screen, one of the finest examples of Renaissance woodwork in all of Europe. The handiwork, credited simply to "Philip the Carver," was a gift to the college from King Henry VIII, and the initials "H" for Henry and "A" for Anne Boleyn can be seen intertwined, as if in a passionate embrace. The screen was certainly created sometime between 1533, when Henry married Anne, and 1536, when he had her beheaded. On the screen's opposite side is an intricately carved panel depicting St. George slaying the dragon.

The lectern, located atop the church's altar, was a gift from Robert Hacomblen, King's College's provost from 1509 to 1528.

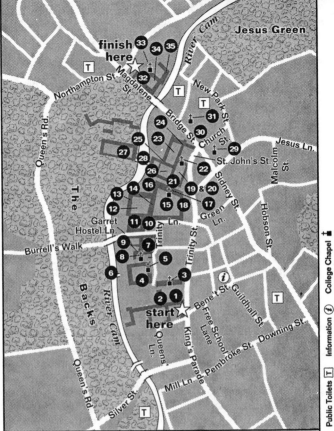

200 m / 220 y

N

River Cam

Jesus Green

finish here

Northampton St.

Magdalene St.

Bridge St.

New Park St.

Church St.

Jesus Ln.

Malcolm St.

St. John's St.

Sidney St.

Green Ln.

Hobson St.

The Backs

Queen's Rd.

Garret Hostel Ln.

Burrell's Walk

Trinity Ln.

Trinity St.

River Cam

Queen's Rd.

Silver St.

start here

Queens' Ln.

King's Parade

Bene't St.

Guildhall St.

Free School Lane

Mill Ln.

Pembroke St.

Downing St.

Public Toilets T   Information (i)   College Chapel

1. King's College
2. Fellows Building
3. King's College Chapel
4. Clare College
5. Clare College Chapel
6. Clare Bridge
7. Trinity Hall
8. Trinity Hall Chapel
9. Trinity Hall Library
10. Trinity College
11. New Court
12. Neville's Court
13. Wren's Library
14. Trinity College Hall
15. Fountain
16. King Edward's Tower
17. Trinity College Chapel
18. Gatehouse
19. St. John's College
20. Great Gate
21. Staircase "F"
22. St. John's Chapel
23. The Second Court
24. The Combination Room
25. Shrewsbury Tower
26. The Third Court
27. St. John's College New Court
28. Bridge of Sighs
29. Church of the Holy Sepulchre
30. The Bridge House
31. St. Clement's Church
32. Magdalene College
33. Magdalene College Chapel
34. Magdalene College Hall
35. Pepys Library

6604

Look carefully and you'll see the provost's name emblazoned on the lectern. Note that the chapel has its original stained glass, a rare survival; most stained glass in English churches was destroyed during the Civil War. Continue past the altar to reach the church's most famed jewel—Rubens' *Adoration of the Magi*—beneath the east window. This oil-on-wood painting dates from 1634, and was commissioned as the altar piece for a convent in Louvain, France. The work of art was donated to King's College in 1961, and the chapel's floor had to be lowered to accommodate it. The chapel is open Monday through Friday only, from 9:30am to 3:45pm.

Leave King's College Chapel, walk clockwise around the building and exit the college through the rear gate. Turn left onto Trinity Lane, then left again, through the gates of:

4. **Clare College,** the second oldest in Cambridge, founded in 1326. The college is thought to have been the inspiration of Chaucer's Soler Hall, in *The Canterbury Tales*. The college quickly foundered financially, only to be re-founded in 1338 by Lady Elizabeth de Clare, the wealthy granddaughter of King Edward I. In addition to catering to the gentry, Lady Elizabeth insisted that her school provide free lodging and education to 10 academically gifted poor boys. Lady Elizabeth's coat of arms, featuring black-and-gold teardrops surrounded by a mourning band, can readily be seen around this campus. The design commemorates her three husbands, all of whom died before she was 28 years old.

Some prominent Clare men include Charles Townsend, the 18th-century chancellor of the Exchequer who imposed taxation without representation on the American colonies; and Charles, Earl Cornwallis, who surrendered his army to American troops at Yorktown in 1781.

Just past the inner gate, turn right, walk through the arch, and enter:

5. **Clare College Chapel,** on your right. Built between 1763 and 1769, the chapel is worth visiting if only to view its altar painting, *The Annunciation*. The work was created in 1763 by Cipriani, a founder of the Royal Academy of Art in London, who is best-known for his painted panels on the monarch's coronation coach.

Exit the chapel, turn left, and then right along the pathway. Walk through the arch onto:

6. **Clare Bridge,** the oldest surviving span over the River Cam, dating from 1640. The bridge was designed by Thomas Grumbold, an architect who was paid the paltry sum of 3

shillings (then about $15) for his work. Note the stone balls on either side of the carvings on the bridge—14 in all. If you place your hand around the sixth ball on the left and touch its other side, you'll feel that it's different from the others. It is said that Grumbold purposely made this piece irregular to privately protest his minimal wage—the architect would always know that the bridge had not been completed.

Walk through the gates on the other side of Clare Bridge and you'll be treated to a magnificent view of The Backs of King's College. In his 1883 travel log, *Portraits of Places,* Henry James describes The Backs as "the loveliest confusion of Gothic windows and ancient trees, of grassy banks and mossy balustrades, of sun-checkered avenues and groves, of lawns and gardens and terraces, of single arched bridges spanning the little stream, which . . . looks as if it had been 'turned on' for ornamental purposes." To the right of the bridge, the Fellows' Garden is one of the loveliest in Cambridge.

Retrace your steps to Clare's main entrance, exit through the wrought-iron gate and turn left along Trinity Lane which takes a sudden cobblestoned curve to the right. A short distance ahead, on your left, is:

7. Trinity Hall, a lawyers' college founded in 1350 by William Bateman, Bishop of Norwich. One year earlier, England had been devastated by the Black Death, a plague that wiped out almost a third of the country's population. The bishop began "The Hall of the Holy Trinity of Norwich" in memory of the nearly 700 of his parish priests who succumbed. The college retains the title "hall" which then referred only to the buildings themselves; the word "college" designated those who occupied the halls. Most of Cambridge's other "halls" became "colleges" in the 19th century. However, since there was already a Trinity College, located just up the street, Trinity Hall retained its name to avoid confusion. The school still teaches both canon and civil law.

Enter Trinity Hall via its main gatehouse and turn left halfway along the path. Turn right just before the arch and walk down that path to:

8. Trinity Hall Chapel, Cambridge's smallest church. Licensed in 1352, the building was unspectacularly modernized in the 18th century. It's worth popping your head in if only to see the lovely altar piece *Presentation in the Temple,* by Manzuoli.

Exit the chapel and walk straight ahead onto the pathway. Turn left through the swinging doors, then right, into:

9. Trinity Hall Library, a 16th-century structure featuring Tudor-style brickwork. The sloping, triangular gable was an Elizabethan addition, and the small doorway above the main entrance was once connected to the Master's Lodge, opposite the library. The library's interior contains many antique furnishings, including the original reading desks.

The library's exhaustive collection includes a book by the Dutch humanist Erasmus, published in 1521 by John Siberch, Cambridge's first printer. In 1971, while preparation was being made to commemorate the publication of Cambridge's first book, historical records were discovered indicating that Siberch never repaid £20 that he had borrowed from the university chest. The reigning university printer ceremoniously repaid the 450-year-old debt—but without the 5% compounded interest that amounted to almost £69 billion. The library is usually open to the public only during the school term, Monday through Friday from 10:30am to 12:30pm.

Exit the library, taking note of the building's famous herbaceous border, which was described in 1883 by Henry James as "the prettiest corner of the world." Turn right, and walk along the pathway to the archway located just ahead of you. This old college gateway dates from 1400, and was placed here in 1873. Walk through the gateway, turn right, and continue to the end of this unnamed path to Trinity Lane. Turn left and, after one block, turn left again, onto Garret Hostel Lane and into the back gate of:

10. **Trinity College,** the largest of the Oxbridge Colleges, and the alma mater of many of the world's outstanding intellectuals, including 28 Nobel Prize winners. Established by King Henry VIII in 1546, not long before his death, the College of the Holy and Undivided Trinity has fulfilled the king's wish to be remembered as the founder of England's greatest college.

One of the college's first fellows was Dr. John Dee, a magician who won fame for the startling stage effects he produced for a production of Aristophanes' *Peace* in 1546. William Shakespeare is said to have had Dee in mind when he created the character of Prospero in *The Tempest*.

Walk straight ahead through:

11. **New Court,** where His Royal Highness Prince Charles, the Prince of Wales, lived when he came up to Trinity in 1967.

Continue through the archway, turn right, and walk through the smaller archway to:

12. **Nevile's Court,** named for Thomas Nevile, a master of Trinity in the late 1590s. It was in these Italianate cloisters that Sir Isaac Newton first calculated the speed of sound by stamping his foot and timing the returning echo.

Turn left into the cloisters, follow them around to the right, and climb the stairs to:

13. Wren's Library. In 1673 the school's master, Isaac Barrow, persuaded his friend, architect Sir Christopher Wren, to donate his services to design a new library and supervise its construction. Completed in 1695, the library is considered Cambridge's best example of neoclassical architecture. The building's four exterior statues, created by Gabriel Cibber, are meant to represent Divinity, Law, Physics, and Mathematics.

Inside the library, at the far end, is a statue of Lord Byron by the noted Danish sculptor Bertel Thorvaldsen. The statue was originally intended for placement in Poet's Corner in London's Westminster Abbey, but the abbey's dean refused the work of art, not because of its quality, which is excellent, but because of its subject, a man whom the church considered to be of questionable morals. Even when he was at Trinity, in 1805, Byron was a bit of a mischief-maker. One of the most famous stories recounts that, since undergraduates were forbidden to keep dogs on campus, Byron brought a tame bear to the school and declared that it would "sit for its Fellowship!"

It was here at Trinity that Byron published *Juvenilia*, a poem that was later acclaimed, after it was retitled *Hours of Idleness*. Cambridge life was agreeable to the boisterous poet, who observed "I like College Life extremely. . . . I am now most pleasantly situated in super-excellent rooms, flanked on one side by my tutor, on the other by an Old Fellow, both of whom are rather checks to my vivacity."

While walking the library's aisles, peek under the protective covers of the showcases that hold many literary treasures, from an 8th-century manuscript of the Epistles of St. Paul to the original manuscript of A. A. Milne's *Winnie the Pooh*. (Both Milne and his son, Christopher Robin, were Trinity men). The library is usually open to visitors Monday through Friday from noon to 2pm, and on Saturdays during the term from 10:30am to 12:30pm.

Retrace your footsteps to Nevile's Court and continue straight along the cloisters. Climb the seven steps and turn right through the very small wooden door. The building on your left is:

14. Trinity College Hall, the school's main dining and social hall. Built by Master Thomas Nevile in 1605, the hall is the largest of its kind in Cambridge. At its far end is a huge portrait of Henry VIII, which appears to preside over those of other Trinity men, including poets Lord Byron and John Dryden, and scientist

Ernest Rutherford, who is credited with splitting the atom for the first time at Cambridge's Cavendish Laboratory in 1932.

Walk down the passageway and out through the small wooden door opposite. Descend the steps and continue straight onto the pathway, past the gatehouse on your right. Take your first left down another path, and pause halfway down on your right at:

15. The Fountain, an early 17th-century font that functioned as the area's principal source of water until the 19th century. Water is funneled here from springs located about 1½ miles away, via a conduit that was originally laid by Franciscan friars.

Farther along the pathway you'll arrive at:

16. The Clock Tower, or King Edward's Tower, the first monumental gateway in Cambridge. The tower has been augmented several times since its construction between 1428 and 1432. It was topped by a statue of Edward III in 1601, and the clock was added during the 18th century. The clock has the peculiar feature of striking twice each hour, on the hour—first with a low note then with a higher one. These bells caught the ear of poet William Wordsworth, who describes them in his poem *The Prelude* as a "male and female voice."

It is tradition for undergraduates to attempt to run around the college's Great Court—a distance of 380 yards—during the time it takes for the clock to strike twelve twice—43 seconds. You may recall this ritual from the film *Chariots of Fire*

Turn right just before the clock and enter the building on your left. This is:

17. Trinity College Chapel, built as a tribute to King Henry VIII by his daughter, Mary Tudor. Inside, on your left, is a statue of physicist Sir Isaac Newton holding a prism. Next to him are statues of other famous Trinity men, including poet Alfred Lord Tennyson (since the poet was fond of smoking, Tennyson's pipe is depicted near the statue's base); and scientist, writer, and lawyer Sir Francis Bacon (shown seated, he is looking depressed and bored). Some of Trinity's famous philosophers and scientists, including Bertrand Russell, are commemorated on brass wall plaques.

Exit the chapel and turn right. Turn left at the clock tower, and left again at the old sundial to:

18. The Gatehouse, topped by a statue of King James I, flanked by sculptures of his queen, Anne of Denmark, and his son, Charles. The gatehouse itself was completed in 1535. After walking under it, look up at the statue of Henry VIII. Originally the statue held a scepter in its hand, but some prankster replaced it with the wooden chair leg that you see today. The coat of arms underneath belongs to King Edward III. Beneath that badge are a half-dozen shields bearing the arms of the king's six sons. Notice that one of the shields is blank—a memorial to William of Hatfield who died at an early age.

Turn left onto Trinity Street which soon becomes St. John's Street. One block ahead on your left is the entrance to:

19. St. John's College, or more precisely, "The Master, Fellows, and Scholars of the College of St. John the Evangelist in the University of Cambridge." The school was founded by Bishop John Fisher, who persuaded Lady Margaret Beaufort, the mother of Henry VII, to convert the hospital of St. John's into a college. Although she was convinced of the merit of the plan, Lady Margaret died before she could make provision for its financing in her will and Fisher had to overcome severe obstacles before the college opened in 1516.

Walk through the:

20. Great Gate, which dates from 1516. Above it is a colorful statue of St. John with an eagle at his feet, a symbol which appears frequently throughout the campus—on gateposts, documents, and even crockery. Lady Margaret's coat of arms is underneath. The curious beasts on either side of the arms are "Yales," mythical beasts with goat heads, antelope bodies, and elephant tails.

Walk along the pathway, at its end turn left. In the corner you will see:

21. A staircase marked "F." This leads to rooms that were occupied by poet William Wordsworth during his undergraduate years, from 1787 to 1791. In his 1850 autobiographical poem *The Prelude,* he describes his rooms and the noise from below:

> *Right underneath, the college Kitchens made*
> *A humming sound, less tuneable than bees,*
> *But hardly less industrious.*

Poke around the courtyard until you find Staircase "G." The curious inscription here reads "STAG Novr 15 1777," and refers to the day a local hunting party chased a stag through the streets of Cambridge and cornered it in this staircase. In the opposite corner of the courtyard is the entrance to:

22. St. John's Chapel, an 1869 structure designed by Gilbert Scott. The original plans called for a spire to top the structure. But an influential graduate felt this was not sufficient, and pledged £1,000 a year for five years to build a full-fledged tower instead. Unfortunately, the donor was killed in a railway accident just two years later, so the college was left to fund the remainder of the project. The chapel itself is as spacious as it is gloomy, darkened by stained glass that is quite spectacular.

Exit the chapel and turn right. At the end of the path, turn right again, climb the three steps, and walk through the passageway to:

23. The Second Court, a conventional Tudor-style brick court-yard. The tower on your left once contained the chambers of James Wood, an early 19th-century St. John's master who bequeathed £20,000 for the construction of St. John's Chapel. When he entered St. John's as a young boy, Wood was rather poor. He was given accommodations in the attic of this tower. Sitting on a top-floor stair with his feet wrapped in straw, the young Wood studied by the weakest light; candles being beyond his financial means. According to legend, Wood's ghost still haunts this building's staircase.

On the second floor of the building on your right is:

24. The Combination Room, used during World War II as a war room that once contained a model of Europe used for military planning and the briefing of senior officers. U.S. General Dwight Eisenhower, English Field Marshal Lord Montgomery, and other top strategists met here to plan part of the D-Day landings. Unfortunately, the room is not open to the public.

Walk along the pathway and turn left. Ahead of you is the:

25. Shrewsbury Tower, a residential building, above which is a statue of Mary, Countess of Shrewsbury, dating from 1671. The tower was named for her in return for donating most of the money needed to build the Second Court.

Walk under the tower and you're in:

26. The Third Court, dominated on the right by the library, dating from 1624, and on the other three sides by buildings dating from 1669 to 1672. Some of the rooms facing this courtyard were set up as an observatory that was used from 1765 to 1859. John Couch Adams, an astronomer who studied here, went on to predict from his observations that another planet must exist beyond Uranus. Subsequently the planet was discovered and named Neptune.

Walk through the round archway, up the ramp on your right, and cross Kitchen Bridge over the River Cam. This brings you to:

27. St. John's College New Court, created by a Neo-Gothic-style building constructed between 1825 and 1831 by architects Thomas Rickman and Henry Hutchinson. Built atop reclaimed marshlands, the building's firm foundations are secured by massive cellars designed to support the four stories above. The result is an extremely attractive building of which Hutchinson was justifiably proud. It is said that the architect was so jealous of his design that he once raced up a staircase to reprimand an undergraduate for sitting in a window, thereby spoiling the building's symmetry!

Return across Kitchen Bridge, stopping in the middle to look left at:

28. The Bridge of Sighs, erected in 1831, which Queen Victoria once called both "pretty" and "picturesque." It is fair to say that the only similarity between this bridge and its famous Venetian namesake is the name.

Walk through the wrought-iron gates on the other side of the bridge and turn left through the passageway to The Third Court. Turn right and return to the college's main gate. Turn left out of the gate onto St. John's Street and walk one long block to the ancient:

29. Church of the Holy Sepulchre, or Round Church, constructed around 1130 by the Fraternity of the Holy Sepulchre, one of a number of small bands of Austin Canons (Dominican friars) that flourished around that time. The church's Norman-style pillars are its most impressive features. Also notable are the carved angels in the chancel—the area surrounding the altar—which date from the 15th century.

A tablet on the church's north wall commemorates the death of Dr. Samuel Ogden, the church's vicar from 1753 to 1761. Typical of 18th-century academic clergyman, Ogden was both a heavy eater and drinker. Although one of his contemporaries described him as "a large black scowling figure. . . ." Ogden was popular; his eloquent sermons attracted members of the university in large numbers. The great English lexicographer Samuel Johnson was also impressed, once remarking "I would like to read all that Ogden has written." Politically ambitious, Ogden was continuously driven by his desire for promotion in both the university and the church. He was so persistent that, in 1764, the vicar succeeded in getting himself elected professor of geology, despite having no geological knowledge nor any intention to teach.

Exit the church and turn right onto Bridge Street. Half a block on your right is:

30. The Bridge House, 16A Bridge Street, one of Cambridge's last-remaining 16th-century buildings. The house's cantilevered design is typical of those that used to exist all over town.

A few doors down is:

REFUELING STOP **The Mitre Tavern,** Bridge Street (no phone). Founded in 1574, the tavern's walls are adorned with a variety of college mottos. It's a nice, atmospheric, low-ceiling pub offering good lamb stews served with crusty bread. Generous portions of pies and other English foods are also served.

Exit The Mitre Tavern and continue along Bridge Street. Two blocks ahead, on your right, is:

31. St. Clement's Church, which dates from the late 12th century. The church's tower was built in 1821 with funds donated by the Reverend William Cole. On the side of the tower facing Bridge Street is the inscription *"Deum Cole,"* a Latin pun meaning "Worship God" and also honoring the tower's patron.

If you walk around the church, you will see the Old Vicarage, an interesting timber-framed house dating from about 1600. Otherwise, continue on about four blocks along Bridge Street and walk over the Bridge Street Bridge onto Magdalene Street. After one block, turn right, into:

32. Magdalene College (pronounced *mawd-len*). Concerned that young men from his religious order should be properly housed and supervised during their studies at Cambridge, the Abbot of Crowland founded a school here called Monk's Hostel in 1428. Rules were stricter than at other Cambridge schools; for example, it was stipulated that "students of this college are to visit taverns less often than other students." Before long other abbeys joined Monk's Hostel. New construction began under the patronage of Henry II and the Duke of Buckingham, and the name was changed to Buckingham College. After Henry VIII's dissolution of the monasteries in the 1530s, the king's chancellor, Thomas Baron Audley of Walden, re-founded the school as the College of St. Mary Magdalene.

Walk through the gatehouse and continue straight along the pathway. Take the first left, and at the end of that pathway, turn right, into:

33. Magdalene College Chapel, a small church that's worth a quick peek before exiting back out to the passage. The small statue in the passage is of Henry VI at the age of 7.

Exit the chapel and turn left onto the pathway. Turn left, under the coat of arms, through the two swinging doors. On your left is:

34. Magdalene College Hall, built in 1519 and enlarged in 1714 when the unique double staircase to the gallery was installed. This was the last hall built in Cambridge designed to be lit exclusively with candles.

Continue along the passageway and enter the next courtyard. The building directly ahead of you, marked by the inscription "Bibliotheca Pepysiana 1724," is:

35. The Pepys Library, built to house the private book collection of 17th-century naval chief and diarist Samuel Pepys (pronounced *peeps*). The library was first bequeathed to Pepys' nephew, then to his old college "entire in one body . . . for the benefit of posterity." The gift consisted of over 3,000 volumes, including the six volumes of Pepys' own famous diary, written in a secret shorthand that allowed Pepys to write freely and candidly about events, people, and the manners of his day. The Reverend John Smith of St. John's College labored for three years to decipher the code, only to find a complete key located in the library. The library is open October 5 to December 4 and January 11 to March 12, Monday through Saturday from 2:30 to 3:30pm. It's open the rest of the year Monday through Saturday from 11:30am to 12:30pm and again from 2:30 to 3:30pm.

Return to the college's main gate and turn left onto Magdalene Street. Continue straight to return to the center of Cambridge.

WALKING TOUR 3

Oxford Part I

Start: The Church of St. Mary the Virgin, High Street.
Finish: The Church of St. Mary the Virgin, High Street.
Time: 2½ hours, not including rest stops.
Best Times: Weekdays from 2pm to 5pm, when all the college buildings are open.
Worst Times: Mornings and Sundays, when many of the colleges are closed to the public.

Oxford University's legendary founder was King Alfred the Great—a tradition that was accepted up to the 19th century. In fact, the university grew up gradually. Scholars were teaching in Oxford, perhaps as early as 1090. By 1100, a philosopher named Theobald of Etampes was lecturing here and was widely celebrated as an educator. In 1167, the town experienced an influx of scholars from the University of Paris, which had expelled all its English students and faculty. The first reference indicating an organized university, mentioning a university chancellor, occurs in 1214.

The lack of affordable student housing led to the foundation of several boarding halls where pupils lived and studied under the direction of a master. In 1264, Walter de Merton founded Oxford's first college, which he modestly called Merton College. Colleges were originally intended for graduate students. The protracted nature of medieval university education meant that it took about 16 years to qualify for a doctorate in theology or law. Few students could afford to stay at the university that long at their own expense. By the time New College was founded in 1379, the colleges began to accommodate undergraduates as well.

Oxford's 35 colleges are independent entities, each owning its own buildings, appointing its own principal or master, and administering its own curriculum. To become a student, candidates must be accepted by both the university and by a particular college. To graduate, students must not only fulfill the requirements of their college but must also pass examinations administered by the university. The university is headed by a chancellor, usually a prominent public figure, but is actually governed by a vice chancellor elected from among the members of the colleges.

In the 15th and 16th centuries, learning flourished at Oxford, and classical learning was introduced into the curriculum by such scholars as Erasmus and Thomas More after the turn of the 16th century. During Elizabeth I's reign, it became fashionable for the gentry and aristrocracy to send their sons to Oxford. Science in the 17th century was represented by such men as Robert Boyle, who developed Boyle's law of the expansion of gases, and Christopher Wren, architect and professor of astronomy.

The 18th century saw a diminution of scholarly activity. The historian Edward Gibbon, author of *The Decline and Fall of the Roman Empire,* remarked of his fellow students: "From the toil of reading or thinking or writing they had absolved their conscience." Reform came to the university in the mid-19th century, undertaken by the university itself; new subjects were introduced, research and scientific teaching flourished, and organized games were encouraged for the first time.

Oxford, home to about 12,000 students, is a delightful place to visit. This walk will guide you around some of the town's most enchanting quarters, through many hidden areas that you might have thought would be off-limits to the public.

Our walk begins with a hearty climb up 104 stairs to the top of the tower of:

1. **The Church of St. Mary the Virgin,** located on High Street, right smack-dab in the center of Oxford. The spectacular unobstructed view from the top will put your forthcoming walk into perspective. The church is located right in the middle of more than a dozen colleges, most of which can be seen from here.

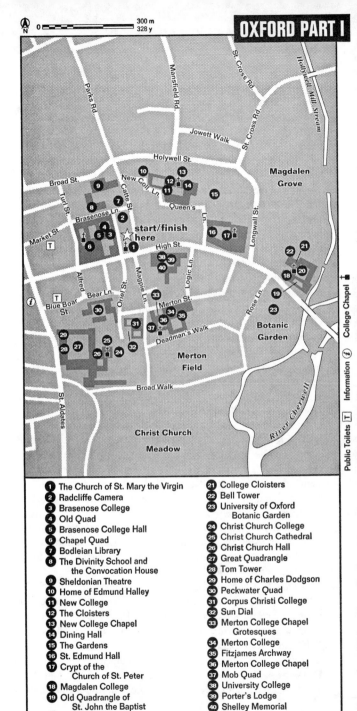

0 ———— 300 m
N   328 y

Parks Rd.

Mansfield Rd.

St. Cross Rd.

Holywell Mill Stream

Jowett Walk

Holywell St.

Broad St.

New Coll. Ln.

Turl St.

Catte St.

Queen's Ln.

Magdalen Grove

Brasenose Ln.

Market St.

Alfred St.

start/finish here

High St.

Longwall St.

Magpie Ln.

Logic Ln.

Bear Ln.

Blue Boar St.

St. Oriel St.

Merton St.

Deadman's Walk

Rose Ln.

Botanic Garden

Merton Field

Broad Walk

St. Aldates

Christ Church Meadow

River Cherwell

Public Toilets [T]   Information (i)   College Chapel ✝

① The Church of St. Mary the Virgin	㉑ College Cloisters
② Radcliffe Camera	㉒ Bell Tower
③ Brasenose College	㉓ University of Oxford Botanic Garden
④ Old Quad	㉔ Christ Church College
⑤ Brasenose College Hall	㉕ Christ Church Cathedral
⑥ Chapel Quad	㉖ Christ Church Hall
⑦ Bodleian Library	㉗ Great Quadrangle
⑧ The Divinity School and the Convocation House	㉘ Tom Tower
⑨ Sheldonian Theatre	㉙ Home of Charles Dodgson
⑩ Home of Edmund Halley	㉚ Peckwater Quad
⑪ New College	㉛ Corpus Christi College
⑫ The Cloisters	㉜ Sun Dial
⑬ New College Chapel	㉝ Merton College Chapel Grotesques
⑭ Dining Hall	㉞ Merton College
⑮ The Gardens	㉟ Fitzjames Archway
⑯ St. Edmund Hall	㊱ Merton College Chapel
⑰ Crypt of the Church of St. Peter	㊲ Mob Quad
⑱ Magdalen College	㊳ University College
⑲ Old Quadrangle of St. John the Baptist	㊴ Porter's Lodge
⑳ Magdalen College Chapel	㊵ Shelley Memorial

6654

Even without the view, however, the pretty church would warrant the climb. Take a look at St. Mary's Church's rooftop gargoyles—carved creatures that were put here to protect the church, both spiritually and physically. The gargoyles not only protect the building from evil spirits but also serve a functional purpose: Rain water collected by the gutters on the roof is funneled out, or gargled, through the sculptures' stone mouths—the word "gargoyle" comes from the old French word *gargouille,* which means "throat."

After your bird's-eye view of Oxford, descend the tower stairs, exit the church through the same door you entered, and turn right onto Radcliffe Square. Then turn right again, down the narrow alley into the center of Radcliffe Square. The rotund building that dominates the square is:

2. **Radcliffe Camera,** a circular-shaped reading room for students. Built between 1737 and 1749 at a cost of £40,000, this camera, or "vaulted chamber," is named for its chief patron, Dr. John Radcliffe, physician to William III and his queen, Mary. Originally called the Physic Library, the building became a simpler study center in 1861, when its collection of books, the nucleus of the Radcliffe Science Library, was moved to the nearby University Museum. Radcliffe Camera is not open to the public.

To the left of Radcliffe Camera is the main gatehouse of:

3. **Brasenose College,** co-founded in 1509 by the Bishop of Lincoln, William Smyth, and lawyer, Sir Richard Sutton. Officially The King's Hall and the College of Brasenose, the school stands on the site of several medieval academic halls. One of these, called "Brazen Nose Hall," was named for an ornate brass 12th-century door knocker—called the Brazen Nose—that used to hang on the building's front door. Such ornate door knockers, collectively known as "sanctuary knockers," were traditionally affixed to doors of church buildings that provided political and spiritual sanctuary to anyone who requested it.

Walk through the college's gatehouse (believed to date from the 16th century), into the:

4. **Old Quad,** a 16th-century group of buildings that are widely acknowledged to be some of the best preserved in Oxford. Upon close inspection, you might be able to tell that the buildings' top floors were added later, in the 17th century. The sundial to your right dates from 1709.

Turn left and follow the pathway around to:

5. **Brasenose College Hall,** an old dining and meeting hall. The weathered busts above the entrance date from the 17th century,

and depict one of England's first kings, Alfred the Great, along with Johannes Erigena, a learned Scot who is said to have lectured here. Walk inside the hall, where a fine ceiling shelters a large fireplace and numerous portraits of former school fellows. At the far end of the hall is the 12th-century Brazen Nose door knocker that gives this college its name. The intricately designed knocker resembles an animal's face, with dog-like ears. Notice its smooth and rounded form. Popular legend holds that undergraduates who committed offenses against the school were forced to sit on the uncomfortable brass knocker as punishment; these centuries-old pants polishings are the visual byproduct.

Exit the hall, turn right down the passageway, then right again, to:

6. **Chapel Quad,** a 17th-century quadrangle with an unusual arcade that leads to a fine baroque chapel you may wish to explore.

Retrace your footsteps to the college entrance and turn left onto Radcliffe Square. Exit Radcliffe Square through the iron gates, cross Brasenose Lane, and walk straight, into Bodleian Library Square. On your left a statue of the Earl of Pembroke, a former university chancellor, stands in front of the:

7. **Bodleian Library,** one of the world's most important book depositories. In size and significance Bodleian Library is second only to the British Library in London. The main rooms are reached through a vaulted passageway in which the library's various publications are displayed. By a 1610 decree, now incorporated into Britain's Copyright Act, Bodleian Library enjoys the right to a copy of every literary work that's published in England. The library is open to visitors, Monday through Friday from 9am to 5pm, and Saturday from 9am to 12:30pm (tel. 0865/277165 for information). It's closed Sunday.

Return to the building's entrance hall and walk through the decoratively molded doorway into:

8. **The Divinity School and the Convocation House,** a college that awards the doctor of divinity degree, which was the highest academic distinction during the Middle Ages. The college's high prestige was matched by superior architecture. Constructed during the 15th century, the school's carved-stone Main Hall was considered spectacular in its day, and remains one of the finest examples of the English Perpendicular style. It survives today virtually intact.

Retrace your footsteps to the building's main entrance and turn left. Walk through the passageway and turn left, entering:

9. **The Sheldonian Theatre,** designed by Sir Christopher Wren

in 1663 as an assembly hall for academic exams and celebrations. One of Oxford University's principal buildings, the Sheldonian was built with its curved back facing the street, enabling the front to face the Divinity School. Wren's design, based on an open-air Roman theater, features a wide, unsupported flat ceiling painted to represent the sky, and simulated ropes that in a Roman theater would have borne a canopy to shade the audience. Behind the painted canopy is a depiction of winged cherubs revealing an allegorical scene in which Truth, Art, and Science conquer Envy, Thievery, and Ignorance.

The enclosed area in front of you is the Proctors Box, an area containing elaborately carved and gilded compartments in which proctors (officials who are responsible for enforcement of discipline) used to sit. The boxes are decorated with gold lion heads, from the mouths of which protrude *fasces*—bundles of elm twigs—the symbol of the Roman magistrate's authority. (The emblem returned in the middle of this century, when Italy's Benito Mussolini adopted the fasces name and symbol for his Fascist Party.)

The Chancellor's Chair sits in the center of the gilded auditorium. Examine the portraits that hang in the theatre's south corner. One is of architect Wren and another is of Archbishop Gilbert Sheldon, the man who commissioned the building.

If you are both willing and able, you can climb to the top of the Sheldonian for another fine view over Oxford.

Exit the theatre, walk clockwise around the building, and cross Catte Street to New College Lane. Walk under the Bridge of Sighs and turn left, into the alleyway called Bath Place. Here you will find:

REFUELING STOP   The Turf Tavern, Bath Place (tel. 0225/243235). A splendid low-ceilinged ale house, The Turf traces its foundations to the 13th century. In 1968, the pub became a favorite haunt of visiting American Rhodes scholar William Jefferson Clinton—better known today as President Bill Clinton.

In addition to traditional, inexpensive "pub grub," served daily until 9pm, the tavern features a good selection of unusual beers, including Castle Eden, Flowers, and the powerful, aptly named Headbanger.

Retrace your steps up Bath Place alley and turn left onto New College Lane. The lime-colored building on your left was the:

10. Home of Edmund Halley, the leading astronomer of the 17th century. Halley (1656–1742) won lasting fame when he predicted the return of the comet that now bears his name. By the time he "came up" to Queen's College, Halley's interest in astronomy was already developed; he arrived with a large collection of instruments, including a 24-foot telescope. After inventing a method for measuring solar eclipses, Halley quit Oxford in 1676 (before earning his degree) and sailed to the South Pacific to study the positions of stars. The astronomer returned the following year, bearing the first-ever map of the southern skies. Although Halley had not fulfilled the university's residency requirements, King Charles II intervened on the astronomer's behalf, and Halley was awarded a master's degree. Halley became a professor of geometry in 1704, and lived in this house from 1705 to 1713 before returning to his permanent London residence.

Continue down curvy New College Lane to:

11. New College, founded in the 14th century by the rich and powerful bishop of Winchester, William of Wykeham, to educate prospective administrators of the church and state. Originally known as St. Mary College of Winchester, the school soon came to be called "New College" to distinguish it from the slightly older House of the Blessed Mary the Virgin (which is now called "Oriel," see Stop 30 in "Walking Tour 4—Oxford Part II").

Enter through the college gatehouse into the Front Quadrangle. Turn left, then left again, into:

12. The Cloisters, a hushed haven dominated by a 14th-century bell tower and an immense tree. Many of the statues that line the cloisters' walls were once perched on the tower of nearby St. Mary's Church.

Walk clockwise around the cloisters to:

13. New College Chapel, one of Oxford's most stunning chapels. The seven-foot statue just inside the antechapel, to your left, is by Jacob Epstein and depicts Lazarus, the biblical brother of Mary and Martha, who is said to have been raised from the dead by Jesus. The Great West Window, above the statue, was painted between 1778 and 1785 by Thomas Jarvis from designs created by Sir Joshua Reynolds, founder of the Royal Society of Arts and celebrated portrait painter. It shows a nativity scene that includes a shepherd that is a likeness of Sir Joshua. Below the nativity are figures representing Christian virtues: Faith, Hope, Charity, Temperance, Fortitude, Justice, and Prudence.

With the exception of the Great West Window, most of the stained glass in this antechapel is more than 600 years old; it was installed as soon as the stone work was finished, around 1386. The scenes and characters on these windows are from Christian history generally—the first three from the Old Testament, the next two from the New Testament, and the last two of later periods.

Continue into the main body of the chapel, past the intricately carved pews, to the left side of the altar. Here, under glass, is a gilded silver crozier, or staff, one of Great Britain's most magnificent examples of 14th-century craftsmanship.

Exit the chapel, turn left, cross the quad, and climb the stairs to the:

14. **Dining Hall,** the oldest extant meeting and eating hall in Oxford. Built in 1386, the hall contains several interesting artifacts, including a screen dating from 1553 and a series of portraits of former fellows.

It's worth seeking out the portrait of the celebrated eccentric William A. Spooner (1844–1930), an unusual-looking albino, with a disproportionately large head. The idiosyncratic Reverend Spooner was famous for mangling sentences; his verbal foibles made "spoonerism" (an unintentional interchange of sounds in two or more words) a legitimate English term. While officiating at a wedding, Spooner reportedly said "It is kistumary to cuss the bride." At the optician's office he asked, "have you a signifying glass?" and upon receiving a negative answer replied, "Oh well, it doesn't magnify." "Sir," Spooner once said to an undergraduate he was disciplining, "You have tasted a whole worm. You have hissed my mystery lectures. You were caught fighting a liar in the quad. You will leave by the next town drain."

After inspecting the dining hall, exit via the left-side door and descend the stairs to the Garden Quadrangle. Walk through the wrought-iron gates on your left, and enter:

15. **The Gardens,** a spacious park surrounded by a section of Oxford's city wall that dates from the 12th century. When the founder of New College obtained this land in the 14th century, he did so with the understanding that the college would assume responsibility for maintaining this part of the city's wall. Although the wall is no longer required for the city's protection,

the college still to this day is obligated to maintain it. Ever the caretaker of tradition, the university hosts a ceremonial inspection of the wall by the Corporation of the City of Oxford every three years. All this attention has paid off: Today, the medieval wall is still in top condition, and its bastions, parapets, and battlements remain largely as they were more than 600 years ago.

Retrace your steps to New College's main entrance and turn left, onto New College Lane, which jogs abruptly left, changes its name to Queen's Lane, then curves to the right. Turn left, through the arched gatehouse, into:

16. St. Edmund Hall, yet another of the dozens of colleges built to house Oxford's medieval scholars. According to university records, there was a structure on this site as early as 1270, but its origins may be even older. Many researchers believe that Edmund Rich of Abingdon, Archbishop of Canterbury, lived and taught on this site in the 1190s. He was canonized in 1248.

Following Henry VIII's dissolution of the monasteries in the 1530s, St. Edmund Hall survived as a semi-independent protectorate of Queen's College until 1957, when it was regranted its own charter. Today, "Teddy Hall," as it is known colloquially, remains physically more modest than its enormous academic stature would lead one to expect.

Just inside the college's front gates turn right into the porter's lodge and ask the porter for the key to the crypt. Turn left, walk through the underpass and ascend the flight of steps fashioned from old tombstones. Turn right at the Church of St. Peter (which now houses the college library and is not open to the public), continue along the pathway and then go left down the stone steps, and use your key to open the locked iron gates of:

17. The Crypt of the Church of St. Peter, which dates from the Norman era, about 1150. Be careful. The crypt is unlighted—a flashlight would come in handy down here. But, even by the low natural light, it's worth looking around this 800-year-old chamber under the church, noting its medieval architecture and designs.

Exit the crypt, making sure that you relock the gates. Retrace your footsteps to the porter's lodge and return the key. Exit Teddy Hall, turn left onto Queen's Lane, then left again onto High Street. About four blocks ahead, on your left, is:

18. Magdalen College, which was founded in 1458. In its 500-year-old charter, the college's name is spelled "Maudelayne" and the name of the college is still pronounced as "*mawd*-len." Almost immediately after the college was built, it attracted many benefactors, and soon became the richest school in Oxford.

Enter the college via the porter's lodge into:

19. The Old Quadrangle of St. John the Baptist, named for a medieval hospital that once stood on this site. To your right is the Canopied Pulpit, a small stage from which an annual sermon has been delivered on St. John the Baptist Day for several hundred years. School records show that in times past, the Old Quad used to be decorated with large tree branches and strewn with rushes to re-create the feeling of a prophet preaching in the wilderness.

Walk to the end of the cobblestone path to:

20. Magdalen College Chapel, a 15th-century house of worship filled with antique glass, pews, and works of art. A magnificent 15th-century bishop's cape is also on display—it's made of green silk and features rich gold embroidery. The cape belonged to the college's founder, the bishop of Winchester.

The stained glass of the chapel's Great West Window depicts the Final Judgment. The chapel's altarpiece, *Christ Bearing His Cross,* was produced in Seville (Spain) in the 17th century, and is thought to be the work of Valdes.

Exit the chapel, turn right, then right again, into the 15th-century:

21. College Cloisters, home to 22 biblically inspired statues. Dating from 1508 and 1509, these exceptional carvings are positioned on pedestals along three of the cloister's four sides. In 1727, antiquarian William Stukely described the sculptures as "whimsical figures" that "amuse the vulgar."

Follow the cloisters counterclockwise to a small doorway on your right. Enter it and walk through the long corridor to:

22. The Bell Tower, a 1509 structure housing 10 musical bells. Famed wit and playwright Oscar Wilde (1854–1900) passed this tower frequently. Wilde entered Magdalen College in 1874 at the age of 20; he later commented that there were two great turning points in his life "the first when my father sent me to Oxford, the second when society sent me to prison." Upon entering Oxford, Wilde immediately began to create his unique image. The young student declared himself a devotee of "art for art's sake" and held numerous "beauty parties" in his rooms, which he had decorated with peacock feathers and objets d'art. Wilde began wearing extravagant clothes, including silk ties and curly-brimmed hats, and established a reputation for witty conversation that often included memorable epigrams like the often-quoted, "Would that I could live up to my blue china." In his third year at Magdalen College, Wilde began to treat his tutors with insolence; although he did well in his studies, the young playwright was already longing for fame and fortune in London. When asked about his plans after school, Wilde replied "God knows; I won't be an Oxford don anyhow. I'll be a poet, a writer, a dramatist. Somehow or other I'll be famous, and if not famous, I'll be notorious." Wilde returned to Oxford periodically, attracted by its intellectual climate and bright young men. It was on one such visit that the writer met Lord Alfred Douglas, the Magdalen student who was to become his lover.

A visiting Rhodes scholar who attended Magdalen in 1958 was Kris Kristofferson.

Retrace your steps to the college's main entrance and turn left onto High Street. One block ahead, on your right, is the:

23. University of Oxford Botanic Garden. Founded in 1621 for the purpose of teaching and research, the garden contains more than 8,000 plant species from around the world. It's open daily from 9am to 5pm.

Exit the gardens, backtrack along High Street, and turn left onto Rose Lane. At the end of the lane continue walking straight, through the gates and past a short avenue of trees. Turn right, onto the gravel pathway called "Dead Man's Walk." Continue for about five minutes along the walk, which jogs left. Turn right into the rear entrance of:

24. Christ Church, another Oxford college. Walk through the 12th-century cloisters of what was once St. Frideswide's Priory, and past the Chapter House, an auditorium that has remained virtually unchanged since its construction in the 15th century. The carved bosses—the projecting ornaments at the intersections of the ribs of the ceiling—and other details of the stonework are worth your close inspection.

Turn right, into:

25. Christ Church Cathedral, the world's only college cathedral. Once inside, turn right again, down the far aisle, where halfway down, on your left, is Nowers' Monument, a perfectly restored effigy of 14th-century knight John de Nowers. Look behind you at the 17th-century Jonah Window, a stained-glass window depicting the biblical story of Jonah and the whale. At the end of the aisle, on your left, is the reconstructed remains of the Shrine of St. Frideswide, patron saint of Oxford, who founded a monastery on the site in Anglo-Saxon times. It was once an important pilgrimage site. Beside the shrine is a rare "watching loft"—a wooden guard's cage from which the shrine could be kept under observation—dating from about 1500.

Turn left, toward the altar, and look at the choir; its vaulting, which dates from 1503, may be the finest example of perpendicular architecture anywhere. Continue past the Military Chapel and turn right. The tomb on your left is Robert King's, Oxford's first bishop.

Exit the cathedral and turn left. Directly ahead is:

26. **Christ Church Hall,** the college's main assembly building. When it was built in 1520 by Cardinal Thomas Wolsey, lord chancellor and archbishop of York, the hall was the largest of its kind in England. Walk up the 19th-century stone stairway, which is protected by an elegant Gothic Revival–style fan-vaulted overhang. Step inside the hall, which is notable for its massive, ornately decorated hammer-beam roof. It is said that the roof was constructed from specially selected Irish oak trees.

During the English Civil War (1642–1646), which pitted the king against Parliament, King Charles I made Oxford his capital, living here in royal fashion for 3½ years. Christ Church Hall hosted most of the king's official functions, including sessions of the monarch's Counter-Parliament. Oxford's strategic position and ample supply of arms and munitions made it ideal as a military headquarters. Eventually, the opposition proved overwhelming, and on April 26, 1646, King Charles I left Oxford for the last time, disguised as a servant. One month later, the town fell in a decisive victory by the Parliamentarians.

Exit the hall and turn right, into the:

27. **Great Quadrangle,** also known as Tom Quad. Financed by Cardinal Wolsey, this quad is Oxford's largest. The buildings around the courtyard were only halfway finished when the cardinal fell out of favor with the king in 1529. When construction was resumed more than 100 years later, builders followed Wolsey's original plans.

The Christ Church Gatehouse, the school's main entrance located directly across from you, is topped by:

28. **Tom Tower,** a belfry designed in 1682 by master architect Christopher Wren. The tower is named for the Great Tom, the largest of its bells. Removed to Christ Church (from an abbey that was dissolved by King Henry VIII in the 1530s), the Great Tom is rung 101 times every night at 9:05pm, once for each of the original members of the college.

The building to the right of Tom Tower was the:

29. **Home of Charles Dodgson** (1832–1898), a mathematics don who is better known by his pseudonym, Lewis Carroll, author of *Alice's Adventures in Wonderland* and *Through the Looking Glass*. Dodgson "came up" to Christ Church in 1851,

was offered a fellowship in mathematics, and stayed here, on and off, for a total of 47 years. For 30 of those years he lived in the building you see now. The academic had no love of teaching, confessing in his diary after only one year on the job that he was "weary of lecturing" and "discouraged." His real interests lay in medicine, word-games, and puzzles, as well as photography, then a nascent art form. Dodgson set up a photographic studio on a roof near Tom Tower where he specialized in portraits of famous people, including Alfred Lord Tennyson. He also liked to photograph little girls, often posed naked. It was one of these little girls—Alice Liddell, the young daughter of the Dean of Christ Church—who became the inspiration for his novel, *Alice's Adventures in Wonderland*. The book was published in 1865. Its huge success surprised the author, who donated much of the profits to various children's hospitals. It is said that Queen Victoria loved the book so much that she asked Dodgson for an advance copy of his next work. Obliging her, Dodgson sent the queen a copy of his subsequent book, *The Condensation of Determinants,* an obtuse mathematical text. The sequel to "Alice," *Through the Looking Glass,* was not published until 1871.

Walk through the archway, past the odd-looking sundial on your left, to:

30. Peckwater Quad, once home to W. H. Auden (1907–1973), one of England's foremost 20th-century poets. Affecting an unconventional air, the poet was often seen wearing an unnecessary monocle or carrying a purely decorative walking cane. In addition to playing Bach on his piano in "Peck Quad," Auden was known to eat at the most expensive restaurants in town, and regularly drank champagne at dog races and boxing matches. Auden left Oxford heavily in debt, but not before publishing several works in the school's journal, *Oxford Poetry*. Auden returned to Oxford in 1956, where he lectured on poetry for five successful years. The poet remained as an informal writer-in-residence, but is said to have been unhappy with the arrangement. Auden died during a summer sojourn in Austria, the day before he was scheduled to return to Oxford.

Continue along the gravel path, and leave the college through the gated archway. Walk straight ahead, onto Merton Street, then turn right, into:

31. Corpus Christi College, a small and prestigious school, founded in 1516 by Bishop Fox of Winchester, and best-known for its emphasis on classical literature.

In the center of the First Quad is the:

32. Sun Dial, a 16th-century timepiece that features a perpetual calendar on its shaft. A refurbishment in 1976 corrected the gnomon—the metal triangle that casts a time-telling shadow—so it now indicates the accurate time.

Retrace your footsteps, exit the college, and turn right onto Merton Street. As you pass:

33. Merton College Chapel, on your right, take a moment and look up at the Merton Grotesques, huge gargoyles protruding from the chapel's north side. These one- and two-headed beasts symbolize demons of the soul that are being expelled from the cold side of the church. As in many medieval European churches, the sunny southern facade is decorated with carved angels warmly welcoming believers.

Directly ahead, turn right, through Merton College Gatehouse into:

34. Merton College, one of the oldest of Oxford's colleges. Founded in 1264 by Walter de Merton, a powerful statesman turned bishop of Rochester, the school's aim was to educate secular priests, many of whom were Merton's own relatives. Celebrated in the 14th century for its progressiveness, the college often took a leading role in the study of astronomy, mathematics, and medicine. Merton graduates include critic and satirist Max Beerbohm (1872–1956) and poet T. S. Eliot (1888–1965). Author J. R. R. Tolkien, the creator of *The Hobbit* and *Lord of the Rings,* lived and taught here during the last years of his life.

Once through the college's main gateway, walk diagonally across the courtyard to the:

35. The Fitzjames Archway, a late 15th-century building that once housed Queen Henrietta during the English Civil War. The fine, vaulted ceiling of the archway features the coat of arms of King Henry VII, surrounded by the signs of the zodiac. The carved symbols, part of the original construction, date from 200 years before astrology and astronomy parted company.

Walk through the arch, turn right into Fellows Quad (ca. 1608–1610), and continue through the archway located just past the clock. Turn right, onto the flag-lined path, to:

36. Merton College Chapel, Oxford's oldest college chapel. Built in the late 13th century, the chapel was originally designed as a traditional cruciform (or cross shape) on the scale of a small cathedral. The nave was never built, however, leaving only a choir, or "top" end, and two transepts, or "arms"—a design that became the model for several other college chapels. The bell tower was added in 1450.

Enter the chapel and take note of the fine East Window,

which contains some original 13th-century glass. The brass lectern dates from 1500, and is considered to be of outstanding craftsmanship. Examine the carvings on the corbels (brackets) that support the pillars on each side of the chancel (the walkway around the pulpit). Dating from the beginning of the 13th century, the carvings are among the oldest in Oxford, and depict "Green Men"—human faces surrounded by leaves and branches that sometimes also emerge from mouths and noses, which are actually a pre-Christian symbol of rebirth and renewal.

Exit the chapel, turn left, and walk through the little archway into the:

37. **Mob Quad,** surrounded by the oldest collegiate building in Oxford, built between 1304 and 1378. Merton College Library, England's oldest, occupies the quad's south and west wings. The library's dormer windows—those that are set upright in the sloping roof—were added during the reign of King James I (1603–1625). Inside the library are some important antiques, and many ancient books and manuscripts. The library is open to visitors most afternoons, but only by guided tour. Visits must be arranged through the curator's office, located in the passageway under the tower. The curator may also allow you to see the room once occupied by writer Max Beerbohm, which now contains some of the essayist's memorabilia.

Exit Merton College through the gate you entered, and turn left onto Merton Street. After one block, turn right onto Magpie Lane, then right onto High Street. Walk half a block, and turn right, through the 17th-century gate, into:

38. **University College.** Founded in 1249, and known locally as "Univ," this is the college where Bill Clinton was enrolled as a Rhodes scholar from 1968 to 1970. The future U.S. president, who was studying for a bachelor's degree in political science, befriended the school's porter and took up a kind of semiresidence in the:

39. **Porter's Lodge,** located just past the gatehouse, to your left. One former Clinton classmate later recalled that the future president and the porter "sat in the porter's lodge, feet by the fire, and turned it into some bizarre version of an Arkansas country store. They were both huge, courageous, very funny, boisterous men, and they harassed literally every under-graduate—Yank or Brit—to come through the door."

With your back to the porter's lodge, walk down the long passageway to the:

40. **Shelley Memorial,** a marble mausoleumlike structure dedi-

cated to Romantic poet Percy Bysshe Shelley (1792–1822). The author of "Ode to the West Wind," "Ozymandias," and *Prometheus Unbound,* "came up" to University College in 1810, having already solidified his eccentric reputation at Eton, where he was known as "Mad Shelley." His antics continued at Oxford, where the poet literally shocked visitors by electrifying his front door, stealing babies right from their strollers, and spilling acid on his tutor's carpets.

While a student at the college, Shelley anonymously co-authored, with his friend Thomas Hogg, a pamphlet entitled "The Necessity of Atheism" that maintained that the existence of God could not be rationally proved. The pair sent the pamphlet to many heads of Oxford's colleges, and to several bishops. Suspected of being the pamphlet's author, Shelley was summoned to an inquiry. He was expelled after refusing to answer any questions.

Percy Bysshe Shelley died in Italy in 1822. This monument to the former student was placed here by the university in 1894, in tardy recognition of his genius.

Exit the college through the gate in which you entered and turn left onto High Street and walk about two blocks to return to The Church of St. Mary the Virgin, the point at which you started this tour.

WALKING TOUR 4

Oxford Part II

Start: Carfax Tower, at the corner of Cornmarket and Queen streets.
Finish: Carfax Tower.
Time: 2 hours, not including rest stops.
Best Times: Weekdays from 2pm to 5pm, when all the college buildings are open.
Worst Times: Mornings and Sundays, when many of the colleges are closed to the public.

The spires of Oxford may be dreaming—as in Matthew Arnold's poem—but the rest of the city is hustle and bustle. In addition to being home to the world's oldest English-speaking university, Oxford is an active industrial city. One of the most attractive things about Oxford is that only a few hundred yards from the bustle and noise of High Street can be found the peace and rural tranquility of the water meadows and the winding Cherwell River.

The university has many traditions, such as the festivities that take place on May Day, in and around Magdalen College. The Magdalen choir, itself a tradition as part of the college's original foundation, sings in Latin from the bell tower at 6am every May 1. Crowds gather to listen in punts from the river, and the ceremony is followed by breakfasting on strawberries and champagne, morris dancing, and bell ringing.

Wedged between the two rivers, the Cherwell and the Thames (known as Isis), Oxford is blessed with dozens of parks and gardens and more than 600 buildings listed for their historical or architectural interest—in short, a perfect place to tour by foot.

Begin your walk at:

1. **Carfax Tower,** the last remaining part of the ancient Church of St. Martin of Tours, located at the corner of Cornmarket and Queen streets. In the 14th century, the church was a bastion of security for the City of Oxford's municipal officers, who retreated to this fortified building during their many confrontations with the town's scholars. The ideologically based battles, which came to be known as "town against gown," often ended with the town leaders hurling objects and abuse at scholars from the top of this tower. University officials protested to King Edward III who, in 1340, ordered the top of St. Martin of Tours' Tower demolished "so that no longer in times of combat would townsmen retire up there as to their castle, to gall and annoy the scholars with arrows and stones . . ." The church's main body was torn down in 1896 to make room to widen busy Queen Street. The tower is open to the public, and provides a fine view over Oxford; there are even free telescopes.

   The building to the right of the tower on Cornmarket Street is:
2. **Abbey House,** a building society (savings and loan) on the site of the Swyndlestock Tavern, Oxford's most infamous medieval pub. It was here, in February, 1355, that one of the town's worst town against gown battles began. Drunken students got into an argument with the pub's landlord, who ended up being beaten about the head with a pot. A riot ensued, and during the next two days, townspeople broke into one college hall after another, smashing objects and beating and killing students. After three days of fighting, the death toll included 63 scholars and an unknown number of townsfolk.

   Although each side was probably equally at fault, a subsequent enquiry found (as was usual) firmly in favor of the university. To punish the townsfolk, King Edward III installed the Oxford University chancellor as administrator of the affairs of the Town of Oxford. In addition to supervising the town's important businesses—which included the checking of weights and measures, and setting the prices of bread and ale—the chancellor's officers were authorized as well to arrest wrongdoers, and try them within the jurisdiction of the university court.

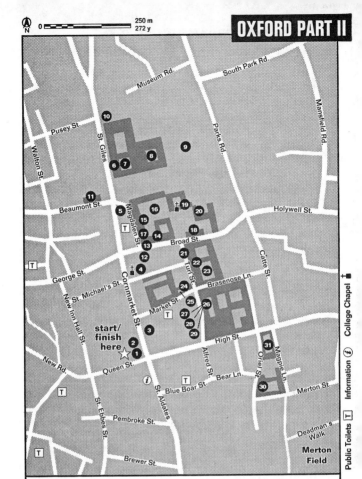

250 m
272 y

0

Museum Rd.   South Park Rd.

Pusey St.

Beaumont St.

Holywell St.

George St.

St. Michael's St.

start/
finish
here

New Rd.   Queen St.

Blue Boar St.   Bear Ln.

Pembroke St.

Brewer St.

Deadman's
Walk

Merton
Field

Walton St.   St. Giles   Magdalen St.   Cornmarket St.   Parks Rd.   Mansfield Rd.   Catte St.   Oriel St.   Magpie Ln.

Broad St.   Turl St.   Brasenose Ln.   Market St.   High St.   Alfred St.   St. Aldates   New Inn Hall St.   St. Ebbes St.   Merton St.

College Chapel ■
Information ⓘ
Public Toilets T

1 Carfax Tower
2 Abbey House
3 Golden Cross Inn
4 Church of
St. Michael-at-the-Northgate
5 Martyrs' Memorial
6 St. John's College
7 Front Quad
8 Canterbury Quadrangle
9 St. John's Gardens
10 St. Giles House
11 Ashmolean Museum
12 The Oxford Story
13 Martyrs' Execution Spot
14 Balliol College
15 Old Gates
16 Garden Quadrangle
17 Rooms of
Aldous Huxley
18 Trinity College
19 Trinity College Chapel
20 Trinity College Hall
21 Turl Street
22 Exeter College
23 Front Quad
24 Jesus College
25 First Quadrangle
26 Lincoln College
27 Lincoln College Hall
28 Kitchen
29 Bust of John Wesley
30 Oriel College
31 Back Quadrangle

6655

For the next five centuries—every year until 1825—the town's mayor, bailiffs, and 63 borough representatives (one for each scholar that had been killed) were forced by university officials to celebrate a solemn mass on the anniversary of the massacre. This humiliating annual ceremony ended when a reigning 19th-century mayor refused to take part in it.

From Carfax Tower, turn left onto Cornmarket Street, then right, onto the small Golden Cross Lane. The Pizza Express just ahead is in the building that was formerly:

3. The Golden Cross Inn, which was here from 1193 to 1988. William Shakespeare often stayed here during his journeys in between London and Stratford-upon-Avon. The landlord, John Davenant, had a wife who was said to be both beautiful and witty and a good conversationalist. One of her sons, the poet Sir William Davenant (1606–1668), later boasted that he was Shakespeare's illegitimate child by Mistress Davenant. In 1927 when some old decorations came to light in the upstairs room, a local newspaper described the chamber as "the room where Shakespeare slept." The room is now the upstairs dining room of Pizza Express; climb the stairs just inside the restaurant if you want to see it.

Return to Cornmarket Street and turn right. Three blocks ahead, on your right, is:

4. The Church of St. Michael-at-the-Northgate, the oldest extant building in Oxford. Constructed in 1020, the church grew wealthy from the offerings of traders who entered the formerly walled Town of Oxford through nearby North Gate. You can climb to the top of the church's steeple, which once doubled as a lookout tower along the town's defensive wall. It's open to the public Monday through Saturday from 10am to 5pm, Sunday from 12:30 to 5pm. The church closes an hour earlier in winter.

Farther along Cornmarket Street, one block past the Church of St. Mary Magdalen, is:

5. The Martyrs' Memorial, commemorating accused heretics Thomas Cranmer (1489–1556), Hugh Latimer (1485–1555), and Nicholas Ridley (1502–1555), all of whom were burned at the stake. The Martyrs, as they are now collectively known, were leaders of the 16th-century English Reformation and of the Church of England; Cranmer was the archbishop of Canterbury, Ridley the bishop of London, and Latimer the bishop of Worcester. The memorial was erected in 1843 and paid for with public donations.

One block ahead, turn right, through the front gatehouse of:

6. St. John's College, known as the College of St. Bernard until 1555. After the college changed hands, the statue that tops the gatehouse was changed, from a depiction of St. Bernard to the likeness of John the Baptist. It is now accompanied by a sculpture of Archbishop Chichele, founder of St. Bernard's.

Walk through the gatehouse and you are in the:

7. Front Quad. Most of the buildings that surround you date from before 1555, when the college was still called St. Bernard's. The building on your left is The Hall, the old refectory (dining hall), built in 1502. Only the vaulted cellars are original; the rest of the structure was rebuilt in the 18th century.

The Chapel, adjacent to The Hall, was consecrated in 1530 and is worth a look inside. School founder Sir Thomas White as well as archbishops Laud and Juxon are buried in the church's sanctuary.

Walk straight through the school's main gate and through the vaulted passageway to:

8. The Canterbury Quadrangle. Directly ahead, enclosed by Renaissance-era colonnades that were completed in 1636, is a statue of King Charles I. Just opposite is a statue of his queen, Henrietta Maria. The gargoyles and grotesques that ornament the roofs around the quad are considered to be the finest in Oxford.

Walk under the statue of Charles I into:

9. St. John's Gardens, a bucolic area that was loved by respected novelist Robert Graves (1895–1985), who was a student at St. John's. Widely admired as both a poet and intellectual, Graves is best known for his historical novels, including I, *Claudius*. Since he was not overly fond of school, Graves welcomed the outbreak of World War I as a chance to escape academia in favor of the armed forces. The writer married in 1918, and returned to St. John's the following year, suffering from shell shock and other scars of war. The couple took up residence on nearby Boar's Hill, in a cottage at the end of poet John Masefield's garden. Graves became a professor of poetry at St. John's in 1961 and proved popular as a lecturer, sometimes packing 2,000 students into a hall designed for 700.

Go back to the college's main gate and turn right onto St. Giles Street. Just past the Lamb and Flag pub is:

10. St. Giles House, 16 St. Giles Street, a neoclassical-style 18th-century house that once served as lodgings for circuit court judges.

Cross the road cautiously, turn left on the opposite side and walk one block to:

> **REFUELING STOP   The Eagle and Child,** 49 St. Giles Street (tel. 0865/58085). Popularly known as the "Bird and Baby," the pub's name refers to designs on the family crest of the earl of Derby, who once owned this land. The earl paid his troops here during the English Civil War.
>
> In the 1940s, J. R. R. Tolkien read from his novel *The Hobbit,* and C. S. Lewis read from his *Chronicles of Narnia* in the pub's "rabbit room." The weekly readings by unpublished authors, usually held on Tuesday mornings began in 1930 and were known as "The Inklings." The pub's most recent claim to fame is the landlady's husband, a one-legged stuntman, who doubled for Peter Ustinov in the film *The Last Remake of Beau Geste.*
>
> In addition to traditional "pub grub," the pub serves Tetley, Burton, and Wadsworths 6X beers, and at least seven malt whiskeys.

Exit The Eagle and Child and turn right down St. Giles Street for about three blocks, turning right onto Beaumont Street, and enter:

11. **The Ashmolean Museum,** Beaumont Street (tel. 0865/ 278000), one of the most important museums in England. The Ashmolean began with an extensive collection of historical artifacts donated to the university by Elias Ashmole. The donation was contingent upon the university's ability to provide a suitable place to house the artifacts, which led to the construction of this building in 1845. Inside are exhibits of Greek, Egyptian, and Asian antiquities and paintings. Highlights of the collection include the "Alfred Jewel" of enamel and crystal set in gold, an example of Anglo-Saxon craftmanship dating from the 9th century; a Stradivarius violin; and the lantern supposedly used by would-be political assassin Guy Fawkes under London's Palace of Westminster (see Stop 1 in "Walking Tour 10—York Part II"). The museum is open Tuesday through Saturday from 10am to 4pm, Sunday from 2 to 4pm.

    Exit the Ashmolean, return to St. Giles Street, and turn right. Turn left onto Broad Street, where half a block ahead, on your right, is:

12. *The Oxford Story,* 6 Broad Street (tel. 0865/728822), a multimedia presentation on the history of Oxford. Visitors are seated at a student-style desk and transported, Disney-style, on a moving coaster through various tableaux depicting important

moments from Oxford's past. It's equally hokey, fun, and educational. *The Oxford Story* is open April through October, daily from 9:30am to 5pm; November through March, daily from 10am to 4pm.

The Oxford Story exits onto Ship Street. Turn right onto Cornmarket Street, then right again onto Broad Street. The small cobblestone cross in the center of the road marks:

13. The Martyrs' Execution Spot. This is where Nicholas Ridley, Hugh Latimer, and later, Thomas Cranmer, all of whom were educated at Cambridge, were burned at the stake after being accused of treason and heresy. The clerics were brought to Oxford in 1554 for the purpose of "exposing the error of their opinions" in a public debate. The main debate centered around whether Christ was physically present in the sacrament—the consecrated bread and wine used in the holy communion—or only embodied in spirit, as the bishops maintained. Each man was allotted one day in which to defend himself. Cranmer was a mediocre debater and Latimer was old and in poor health. Only Ridley, unintimidated by the hostile audience, constructed a strong defense. To no one's great surprise, Latimer and Ridley were condemned and sentenced to be executed. The fate of Cranmer, who was head of the Church of England, was deferred. On the day of the execution, a large crowd gathered. As the fire was lighted, Latimer shouted to Ridley "Be of good comfort, Master Ridley, and play the man. We shall this day light such a candle, by God's grace, in England as I trust shall never be put out." Cranmer wavered in his beliefs in the next months, but in March 1556, he followed his colleagues to the stake, first thrusting into the flames the hand that had signed his recantation.

Continue down Broad Street half a block to:

14. Balliol College, one of Oxford's oldest institutions, founded in 1263. The college's origins go back to John de Balliol who, in 1255, had a land dispute with the bishop of Durham. The king sided with the bishop, and John de Balliol was punished with a public whipping. Balliol was then forced to open a house in Oxford for 16 poor scholars and maintain them at his own expense. Balliol's school remained academically undistinguished until the end of the 18th century, when a change in its acceptance policy raised both its academic level and its prestige. Today, Balliol is one of the most prominent colleges in Oxford.

Walk through the school's gatehouse into the Front Quadrangle and cross to the far left corner. Continue through the passageway to the:

15. **Old Gates,** a 16th-century doorway that is believed to have been scorched by the fires that consumed the martyred bishops. Presumed lost after being removed during a 19th-century restoration, the gates were later found and reinstalled here.

The Old Gates open into the:

16. **Garden Quadrangle,** one of the college's main quads. The quad was well-known to student Graham Greene (1904–1991). The author of *Brighton Rock, The Power and the Glory, The Third Man,* and a host of other thrillers and serious novels "came up" to Balliol in 1922. Although he contributed poetry to various journals and edited a magazine, *Oxford Outlook,* by his own acknowledgement, Greene was "a muddled adolescent who wanted to write but hadn't found his subject." In his autobiography, *A Sort of Life,* the author recalls playing Russian roulette in woods near this quad. After putting the muzzle to his ear and pulling the trigger six different times, Greene decided to give up this particular activity in his "life-long war against boredom." In 1924, while still a student, Greene visited the German embassy in London and offered his services as a propagandist. Later he wrote "I was ready to be a mercenary in any cause so long as I was repaid with excitement and a little risk."

Greene also tells of one particular semester when he stayed drunk every day from morning to night. He joined the Communist Party, and spent lavishly on extravagances that left him heavily in debt. Looking back on his Balliol days, Greene remarked that he was grateful that the school furnished him with a strong head and a tough liver. But Greene was not the first heavy drinker to attend Balliol—the college's students and faculty once had such a reputation for drunkenness that the men of Balliol were dubbed "the sons of Belial," after one of the names of Satan in the New Testament.

Return to the college's main gate. The building just to your left once housed:

17. **The Rooms of Aldous Huxley,** author of *Brave New World, Point Counter Point,* and other novels satirizing aspects of contemporary life. Huxley (1894–1963) suffered from an illness that rendered him virtually blind by the time he arrived at Balliol. For a time, he was able to read with the aid of a magnifying glass, but eventually he was forced to study in braille. Tall and elegant, the author was popular with his contemporaries and enjoyed his studies, once writing to his brother "I should like to go on forever learning. I lust for knowledge, theoretic as well as empirical. . . ." The situation

changed when World War I broke out, and most of Huxley's classmates were conscripted. The daily casualty lists of fellow students made depressing reading, prompting Huxley to write: "This war impresses on me more than ever the fact that friendship, love, whatever you like to call it is the only reality. . . ."

Exit the college and turn left onto Broad Street. Half a block ahead, on your left, is the entrance to:

18. **Trinity College,** originally founded in 1286 by and for Benedictine monks. Purchased from the Benedictines in 1555 by Sir Thomas Pope, an Oxfordshire lawyer who amassed a fortune in the service of King Henry VIII, the school was renamed "The College of the Holy and Undivided Trinity in the University of Oxford."

Enter the college through the front gatehouse into the New Quadrangle.

19. **Trinity College Chapel,** in the quad's near left corner, dates from 1692, and is decorated with outstanding wood carvings that are thought to be the works of master carver Grinling Gibbons.

After visiting the chapel, exit and turn left toward:

20. **Trinity College Hall,** located in the quad's far left corner. Dating from 1620, the hall, which replaced an earlier hall on this site, is one of the least spectacular in Oxford. You may want to look inside if only to see a portrait of Cardinal Newman (1801–1890). A gifted Trinity student at age 15, Newman would later become the charismatic leader of the influential Oxford Movement, an early 19th-century crusade to free the church of state interference. The Oxford Movement not only threatened the authority of the state but also had close ties to Catholicism, earning Newman and his followers considerable condemnation in this decidedly Protestant country. Newman left Oxford in 1846, entered monastical seclusion for three years, and emerged a Roman Catholic. The cardinal returned 32 years later when he was elected Honorary Fellow of Trinity College.

Exit the hall, turn left, and walk through the passageway to view the Christopher Wren–designed Garden Quad. Retrace your steps and leave the college through the main gate. Walk diagonally across Broad Street into:

21. **Turl Street,** an ancient footpath that was once guarded by a gated archway. The street was originally named "twirl" for the twirling, turnstile-like portal that rendered it accessible only to pedestrians; cattle and carts were prohibited. The gate was demolished in 1722.

Walk one block along Turl Street and turn left, into:

22. Exeter College, Oxford's fifth-oldest school, founded in 1314 by Walter de Stapleton, Bishop of Exeter. Richard Burton, one of Exeter's most famous students, arrived in 1944 in a special wartime arrangement with his Royal Air Force regiment. During his six-month stay, the actor gained an impressive reputation for heavy drinking and for his lively anecdotes about his poor Welsh background. A thespian from an early age, Burton acted here in the Oxford University Dramatic Society's production of Shakespeare's *Measure for Measure*—a brilliant performance that was talked about for years afterward. Burton carried a special affection for Oxford and, although it never came to pass, the actor often talked about his desire to return here as an academic.

Exeter is not the most spectacular school in Oxford, but it's enjoyable to poke around to get a feel for the place. Walk through Parmers Tower, the 1432 medieval gatehouse (now the rector's lodge), into the:

23. Front Quad. Exeter Hall, on your right, which dates from 1618, is admired for its original beamed roof and fine Jacobean screen. Exeter Chapel, located opposite the hall, dates from 1854, and is said to have been inspired by the design of La Sainte Chapelle in Paris. The magnificent tapestry, *The Adoration of the Magi,* on the chapel's south wall, was conceived by Sir Edward Burne-Jones and executed by William Morris, both of whom are honorary fellows of the college.

Exit Exeter College and walk diagonally across Turl Street into:

24. Jesus College. Founded in 1571 primarily for the education of Welsh scholars, the school's Welsh connections remain strong to this day.

Walk through the front gatehouse into the:

25. First Quadrangle, which is dominated by Jesus College Chapel, on your right. Built in 1636, the church is not especially noteworthy, but contains a bust of Lawrence of Arabia (1888–1935), an undergraduate here early in this century.

Exit the chapel, turn right, and follow the pathway that leads to Jesus College Hall, in the Inner Quadrangle, before retracing your footsteps to the college gate. Exit Jesus College and turn right onto Turl Street. Cross Brasenose Lane and continue half a block on Turl to:

26. Lincoln College, which is named after its 15th-century founder Richard Fleming, Bishop of Lincoln. Architecturally, Lincoln is more faithful to its medieval roots than any other

Oxford college; no building in the college's Front Quadrangle is less than 500 years old.

Walk straight, into:

27. Lincoln College Hall, taking note of the building's original collar beams (those that protrude from the walls at right angles) and smoke louvre (the pattern that's carved in stone).

Exit the hall, turn right, and walk through the little archway. Notice the battered doorway which is the entrance to:

28. The Kitchen, the oldest part of the college built on the site of an earlier academic hall, mentioned in official records as early as 1300.

Retrace your steps to the Front Quad and turn left. Follow the pathway to:

29. The bust of John Wesley, co-founder (along with his brother, Charles) of the American Methodist movement. Wesley (1703–1791) lived above this passage while studying for his master's degree, which he earned from Lincoln College in 1727. A dedicated evangelist, Wesley was ordained into the priesthood the following year, then recalled to Lincoln in 1729 as a philosophy teacher. At about this time Wesley joined forces with his brother, Charles, who was studying at nearby Christ Church College. Charles had started a small religiously oriented group that came to be known as "The Holy Club." In addition to reading and praying together, the group began to engage in such activities as visiting prison inmates, helping care for the city's poor, preaching to prostitutes, and exorcising demons from houses. The Holy Club's daily practices included waking at 5am, praying each hour, and meditating frequently. The group's fanaticism soon drew ridicule from fellow students, who dubbed them "Methodists" in mockery of their zealous adherence to routine.

In 1735, John and Charles Wesley left Oxford for America to do missionary work in Georgia.

Return to the main gate and exit Lincoln College, turn left onto Turl Street, then right onto High Street. Just ahead, on your right, you'll see:

REFUELING STOP   The Mitre Tavern, High Street (tel. 0865/244563). The property of Lincoln College since the 15th century, The Mitre is one of Oxford's most historic pubs; parts of it date back to Saxon times. The pub serves hearty meals that include steak, chicken, and other substantial dishes.

Exit The Mitre and turn left onto High Street. Three blocks ahead, turn right onto Oriel Street and walk another long block to:

30. Oriel College, Oxford's sixth-oldest college, founded under the patronage of King Edward II in 1324.

Walk through the main gatehouse, cross to the far left corner of the 17th-century Front Quadrangle, and walk through the small passage to:

31. The Back Quadrangle, an 18th-century courtyard that's home to the school's Palladian Library. It was here that financier, statesman, and empire builder Cecil Rhodes (1853–1902) studied for eight years, beginning in 1873. One of the founders of modern South Africa, Rhodes had already established himself as a successful businessman by the time he fulfilled his ambition to attend Oxford. He entered Oriel College after being refused admission to nearby University College. A determined scholar who read voraciously, Rhodes alternated between the life of a student and that of a businessman, making several trips to Africa between periods of study. Rhodes led a secluded life, attended few lectures, and did not socialize much with the younger students, to whom he appeared cynical and worldly.

The millionaire South African government minister remembered his alma mater in his will, bequeathing £100,000 to Oriel and establishing a foundation that still provides 160 scholarships to Oxford each year—two from every state in the United States and three from each of Britain's 18 current and former colonies.

Return to Oriel's main gate, exit the college and turn right onto Oriel Street. Turn left onto Bear Lane, then right onto Alfred Street (if you'd like to take a last break) to:

FINAL REFUELING STOP The Bear Tavern, Alfred Street (tel. 0865/244680). Boisterous and frequently crowded, The Bear is the quintessential students' pub, dating from 1242. College rugby players regularly celebrate victories here and have, on occasion, been known to put their heads through the low ceiling. The pub is also known for its unique pewter bar and its collection of nearly 5,000 wall-mounted ties. More important is The Bear's reputation for serving the best-value pub food in Oxford.

Exit the pub, continue to the end of Alfred Street, then turn left onto High Street. One long block ahead is Carfax Tower, the point at which you started this tour.

WALKING TOUR 5

Bath Part I

Start: Bath Abbey.
Finish: The intersection of John, Wood, and Quiet streets.
Time: 1½ hours, not including rest stops.
Best Times: Daily between 9am and 5pm.
Worst Times: Early morning and early evening, when many of the major sights are closed.

Bath's mineral spring has been an attraction for almost 2,000 years.
Each day, over a half-million gallons of thermal mineral water—naturally fortified with a mixture of sodium, magnesium, lime, sulphate of soda, and carbonic acid—gushes from these grounds at temperatures hovering around 118° Fahrenheit (48° Celsius).

The area is believed to have been known for its curative spring as far back as the Bronze Age. The legend is that Bladud, son of an ancient king, was banished from his father's kingdom, suffering from leprosy. He found employment herding pigs, but the pigs contracted his disease. To avoid the pig-owner's wrath, the prince fled into the woods where the pigs found and frolicked in pools fed by the hot spring. Soon afterward, Bladud noticed that the pigs' leprosy began to diminish. The prince stripped naked, bathed in the hot muddy water, and was himself cured. He afterward built the city of Bath. Bladud, incidentally, had a son Lear, who was immortalized in Shakespeare's play.

The real story of Bath is only slightly less colorful. When the Romans, who conquered England in A.D. 43, encountered the spring dedicated to Sul, Celtic goddess of healing whom they identified with their own goddess, Minerva, they built a temple to Sul-Minerva adjacent to the spring. The town that grew up around the temple was known as Aquae Sulis or "Sul's Spa," and is thought to have attracted visitors from throughout Europe.

After the Roman legions were recalled from England in the 4th century, Sul's Spa, renamed "Hoete Bathum" by the Saxons, gradually declined into ruin. For the next few hundred years, monks were the primary inhabitants. Reports of cures became commonplace.

The Bath we see today is the result of the vision of three men—socialite Richard "Beau" Nash, venture capitalist Ralph Allen, and architect John Wood—who rebuilt it to magnificent proportions and made it a center of 18th-century society. John Wood the Elder and his son John based Bath's design on the hills of Rome, and we can see the realization of his idea in the harmonious rise of its Georgian crescents that were constructed from the local, gold-tinted stone. By the late 18th century, Bath could easily support its claim as one of England's most beautiful cities.

Unfortunately, Bath was heavily damaged in World War II. Since that time, the city has undergone a painstaking restoration. Bath is an extraordinarily beautiful town, and one of the most popular excursions from London.

Start your tour at the end of High Street, in front of the west side of:

1. **Bath Abbey,** the city's most important church. A church has stood on this site since A.D. 937, when King Edgar, the first English king, was crowned here. The abbey is the third to be built on this site. It was commissioned in the 16th century by Oliver King, who was both bishop of Bath and secretary to King Henry VII.

   Something of a mystic, King ordered the abbey's construction after he had a dream about an olive tree, a ladder, and a gaggle of angels. In his dream, a heavenly voice cried out "Let an olive establish the crown, let a King restore the church." King understood this to mean that he was being called by name to support the Tudor cause and rebuild the abbey. The story of

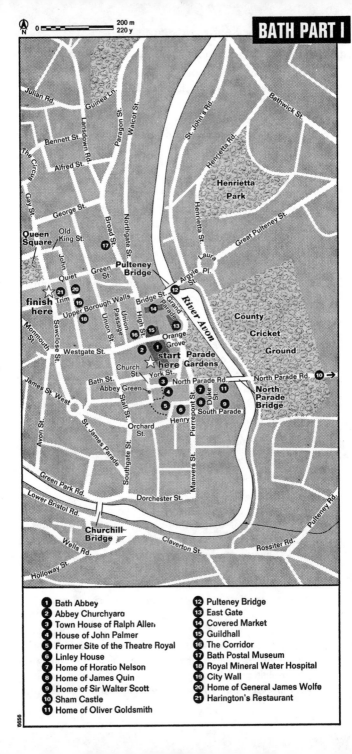

0 — 200 m
— 220 y

1 Bath Abbey
2 Abbey Churchyard
3 Town House of Ralph Allen
4 House of John Palmer
5 Former Site of the Theatre Royal
6 Linley House
7 Home of Horatio Nelson
8 Home of James Quin
9 Home of Sir Walter Scott
10 Sham Castle
11 Home of Oliver Goldsmith
12 Pulteney Bridge
13 East Gate
14 Covered Market
15 Guildhall
16 The Corridor
17 Bath Postal Museum
18 Royal Mineral Water Hospital
19 City Wall
20 Home of General James Wolfe
21 Harington's Restaurant

6656

King's dream is depicted in a sculptural frieze on the side of the abbey that you are now facing.

The statue over the church's west door is of Henry VII, and on either side of the door are statues of St. Peter and St. Paul, to whom this abbey is dedicated.

Bath Abbey was the last of England's big churches to be built in the Perpendicular style, the third and last English Gothic style, characterized by vertical ornamental lines. Stone masons William and Robert Vertue began the building in the mid-16th century with plans for a magnificent fan-vaulted roof. Work had only reached the church's transept—the point just under the tower—when King Henry VIII abolished monasteries and abbeys and appropriated all church lands in 1539. The unfinished building was pawned off on the City of Bath in 1572.

Enter the abbey and turn left. Walk along the monument-lined wall past the third column on your right, to the tomb of James Montagu, Bishop of Bath from 1608 to 1615. Once when the bishop was out walking with his friend, Sir John Harington, it began to rain heavily and the two ducked into the church, which was still roofless. Soaking wet, Sir John commented, "If the church does not keep us safe from the water above, how shall it save others from the fire below?" Bishop Montagu immediately ordered the construction of a wooden roof. Bishop Montagu's roof was added in 1614 and remained in place until the construction of the present fan-vault roof in 1869.

The effigy of James Montagu lies on a slab of black "touchstone," a type of rock once used to test the quality of gold and silver by the streak left on the stone when the metal was scraped against it.

Continue to the top of the aisle to the James Quin Monument, a memorial to an 18th-century thespian who was a Shakespearian actor and a friend and rival of actor David Garrick. Quinn's grave is inscribed:

> *The scene is changed, I am no more*
> *Death's the last act. Now all is o'er.*

Look inside the abbey's small chapel, and find the monument to Mary Frampton (d. 1698) located above the Golden Eagle. Little is known about Frampton, but the monument is noteworthy for its epitaph, a short poem that was written for his tomb by poet John Dryden. No one knows the connection between

Frampton and Dryden, but since this poem appears in all the collections of the poet's work, we might consider the inscription here a first edition!

The side aisle of the abbey contains a memorial to Lady Waller (d. 1633), the wife of Sir William Waller, commander of the Parliamentary forces against Royalists in the 1643 Battle of Lansdown. Notice the physical damage and graffiti on the tomb's effigy. This centuries-old vandalism by supporters of the king was remarked upon in the famous 17th-century diary of Samuel Pepys.

Exit the abbey and walk straight ahead into the:

2. **Abbey Churchyard,** that 17th-century novelist Daniel Defoe described as a place of "raffling, gaming, and levity." Minus the raffling and gaming, Defoe's description still holds true. Jugglers, musicians, and other street performers often entertain in this charming history-laden yard.

Walk counterclockwise around the abbey, through the alley between the abbey and the ruins of Roman Baths, onto Kingston Parade, a square where the lodgings of the abbey's prior once stood. Bear left across the square and turn left onto York Street. About one block ahead, turn right through the narrow alleyway entrance into the former:

3. **Town House of Ralph Allen,** York Street. Allen, an 18th-century English postmaster and venture capitalist, is credited with the building of modern-day Bath. The son of a Cornish innkeeper, Ralph Allen came to Bath at age 18, got a job at the post office, and meteorically rose to the rank of postmaster within a year.

Allen, it seems, had a habit of opening other people's mail, and one of the letters he covertly read told of an imminent Jacobite rebel attack being planned in the West Country. Allen warned the king, and the attack was quashed before it even began. Allen's career blossomed. As postmaster he reorganized and improved England's postal system. He invested in stone quarries at nearby Combe Down, and working his connections, was instrumental in the movement to rebuild Bath. He then sold the town's builders rock from his Combe Down quarries.

When his town house was built, it enjoyed magnificent views of the nearby river and surrounding hills. You have to use your imagination—today the building is hemmed-in by shops and office buildings. Often overlooked by tourists, the Town House of Ralph Allen is one of the city's best secret gems.

Retrace your steps along York Street and turn left onto

Church Street. At the end of Church Street is Abbey Green, which was once used by the abbey's monks as a bowling green. Turn left onto North Parade Passage and walk two blocks to:

REFUELING STOP Sally Lunn's House, North Parade Passage. This bakery is located in the oldest house in Bath. The shop gained fame early in the 18th century, when it became the regular morning hang-out of Bath's socialite builders Beau Nash and Ralph Allen.

According to tradition, Sally Lunn, a Huguenot refugee, came to work in this bakery as an employee in 1680. Lunn's adaptation of the recipe for the French brioche, which she brought from France, was so popular that the shop became the favorite meeting place of Bath society, and it wasn't long before the name "Sally Lunn" became synonymous with the bun. The chief evidence against this popular story is the fact that, in France, this sort of bun has always been known as a "Sol et Lune," or "sun and moon," named for its gold top and white bottom.

The Sally Lunn buns that are sold here today are made from the original 17th-century recipe, which was supposedly rediscovered in the 1930s, hidden behind a panel over the fireplace.

Once inside the bakery, it is worth making the descent into the cellar where you will find the smallest museum in Bath and the floor of a Roman-era house that once stood on this site.

Back upstairs, enjoy a cup of tea and a fresh Sally Lunn.

Exit Sally Lunn's, turn left, then immediately right onto North Parade Buildings. The bricked-up doorway on your left was the main entrance to the former:

4. **House of John Palmer,** a theater owner who by chance became a postal service pioneer. In order to get the most out of his actors, Palmer (1741–1818) transported the players between his theaters in Bristol and Bath on a daily basis. This meant that both cast and costumes could appear at both theaters in the same play on alternate nights. Searching for other uses for his regular transport route, Palmer began the first national mail-coach system.

Continue walking about half a block farther on North Parade Buildings and turn right into a passageway that leads to Abbey Green. Walk under the archway in the far left corner of the green and turn left, along the passageway closest to Marks and Spencer department store. Turn left again, onto Old Orchard Street, where one block ahead is the former site of the:

5. **Theatre Royal,** the first royally sanctioned theater built outside of London. It was from this theater that John Palmer ran his shuttle back and forth to Bristol in order to get the most play for his pound.

The Theatre Royal relocated in 1805; the building you see is now the Freemasons Hall.

Continue along the street and turn right onto Pierrepont Place. Just ahead is:

6. **Linley House,** former home of one of Bath's most important 18th-century families. The family's patriarch, Thomas Linley, was artistic director of the city's most popular concerts. Linley's daughter Elizabeth was a gifted singer who was even better known for her outstanding beauty. Two of England's most famous artists, Thomas Gainsborough and Sir Joshua Reynolds, painted her portrait. It was known that a duel had been fought over Miss Linley and, according to Horace Walpole, even King George "ogled her at an oratorio." In the end, Elizabeth fell in love and eloped with an impoverished young playwright Richard Brinsley Sheridan (1751–1816). Within a few years of their marriage Sheridan became famous and Elizabeth contracted tuberculosis and died, at the age of 38.

Walk through the archway and turn left onto Pierrepont Street. Just ahead is the former:

7. **Home of Horatio Nelson,** 2 Pierrepont Street. Nelson (1758–1805), then a junior officer in the navy, came to Bath after serving for 30 months in the Caribbean. This long tour had left him sickly and weakened, so Nelson came to Bath to "take the waters" under the medical direction of a local doctor. In 1781 Nelson wrote to a friend, "My health, thank God, is perfectly restored although I shall remain here a few weeks longer, that it may be firmly fixed, as also to avoid the cold weather, which I believe is setting—for you know, this is like Jamaica to any other part of England."

Backtrack along Pierrepont Street and pause outside the former:

8. **Home of James Quin,** 3 Pierrepont Street. An actor and noted wit, Quin (1693–1766) was considered to be the finest portrayer of Shakespeare's character Falstaff on the stage. The actor lived in this house for the last 15 years of his life, moving from London after heated quarrels with his manager. Regretting the arguments, Quin sent the manager a brief message that read "Am in Bath." The embittered manager's equally brief reply

read "Stay there and be damned." Quin loved Bath, frequently referring to it as "a fine slope to the grave." Quin, who was known to drink heavily at a nearby pub called The Pelican, once quipped, "They call it 'The Pelican' because of the size of the bill."

Turn left, onto South Parade, where a wall plaque marks the former:

9. Home of Sir Walter Scott, 6 South Parade. Scott (1771–1835), author of *Ivanhoe, The Heart of Midlothian,* and many other novels, came to Bath at age 4, brought by a doting aunt who hoped the town's healing waters would cure the youngster's pronounced limp, a result of childhood polio. The therapy didn't work and the limp remained permanent.

Continue to the end of South Parade, and look up at what appears to be a castle on the hillside in the distance. This is in fact:

10. Sham Castle, the false facade of a non-existent palace. The castle front was erected by Ralph Allen (see Stop 3, above) for the sole purpose of enhancing the view from his town house.

Retrace your steps along South Parade, turn right onto Duke Street, then left onto North Parade. Pause outside the:

11. Home of Oliver Goldsmith, 11 North Parade. Goldsmith (1728–1774), the perennially cash-strapped author of *The Vicar of Wakefield* and *She Stoops to Conquer* and biographer of visionary Beau Nash, arrived in Bath at the age of 34 with the dream of writing a money-making book. The answer was a brutally frank tell-all biography of Nash—a book that summarized the socialite as an old despot who "went to the very summit of second-rate luxury." Of Nash's wit, Goldsmith commented: "Of all the jests recorded of him I scarce find one that is not marked with petulance . . . once a week he might say a good thing." And of Bath itself, Goldsmith astutely commented: "Bath came into vogue because people of fashion had no agreeable summer retreat from London and usually spent that season amidst a solitude of country squires and parsons' wives . . . they wanted some place where they might have each other's company and win each other's money, as they had done during the winter in town."

Backtrack along North Parade, cross Duke Street, and continue straight onto North Parade Bridge. Pause in the center of the bridge and look left, up river, at:

12. Pulteney Bridge, a 1771 span designed by architect Robert Adam. It was inspired by the shop-lined Ponte Vecchio in Florence, Italy.

Cross the River Avon, turn left and go down the narrow staircase, then turn right and walk along the riverbank past the Garden Maze. Keep left, on the little walkway that heads towards the river. Climb the stairs, turn left, then left again, into Argyll Street. Recross the river on Pulteney Bridge, then turn left onto Grand Parade. After two blocks, turn right onto the somewhat disheveled Boat Stall Lane. On the other side of the railings to your left, a descent leads to:

13. East Gate, one of the ancient entrances in the medieval wall that once surrounded Bath. This was the arrival point for people and cargo arriving in the city by riverboat, and the stone gateway and its surrounding walls have been scored by the ropes that were once used to hoist objects from the boats below.

Continue along Boat Stall Lane and bear right, into:

14. The Covered Market, an 18th-century meat market. Turn left inside the market toward the large stone in the middle of the floor. This is The Nail, the place where traders once did their haggling. When a deal was agreed upon, the buyer counted his money out on The Nail. This practice led to the colloquial expression "cash on the nail."

Walk to the end of the market, exit onto High Street and turn left. Walk half a block to:

15. Guildhall, the chief meeting hall for the city of Bath in the 18th century. After the building's foundation was laid in 1768, a disagreement over the architect's design halted construction for eight years. Construction was continued in 1776, and upon completion, Guildhall opened to raves—the building really was spectacular. Enter the building and walk up the stairs to the second-floor banqueting hall, a room that many critics agree is one of the finest public rooms in England. Notice the ornate chandelier, which is composed of some 15,000 pieces. Purchased in 1778 at a cost of £270, the light fixture was apparently less than perfect upon delivery—city fathers deducted 3 shillings off the final bill.

Exit Guildhall, turn right, then left, into:

16. The Corridor, one of Bath's first shopping malls. Inside, at number 7, is the former studio of William Friese-Green (1855–1921), the inventor of cine-photography. Friese-Green was the first person to produce sensitized celluloid ribbon, the negative base that makes moving pictures possible. Born in Bristol, the inventor moved to Bath after serving as an apprentice to a portrait photographer. It was in Bath that Friese-Green met and worked with John Arthur Rudge, an inventor who had created moving pictures on a revolving drum. Friese-Green moved to

London in order to market his new invention, but in the big city the inventor ran into debt, leaving others to claim the fortunes that were to be made from moving pictures.

Return to High Street, turn left, and continue straight onto Northgate Street. Turn left onto Broad Street, and walk straight to:

REFUELING STOP The Saracens Head Inn, Broad Street (tel. 0225/426518). This delightful old-world inn has changed little since the spring of 1835 when Charles Dickens lodged here. As a London-based newspaper man working for the *Morning Chronicle,* Dickens came to Bath to report on a speech given by Lord John Russell. It was here that the young Dickens, trying to think of a name for the protagonist of his first novel, saw the name of Moses Pickwick emblazoned on the sides of the coaches that Pickwick operated. Dickens named his first novel *The Pickwick Papers,* and the rest of his literary career is history.

The Saracens Head serves good English pub food Monday through Friday from noon to 2pm, and again from 5:30 to 8:30pm; Saturday from noon to 3pm; and Sunday from noon to 2pm. Their selection of beer includes Courage Best, John Smith, and Directors.

Exit the pub, turn right, and walk a few steps to the:

17. Bath Postal Museum, 8 Broad Street. The first stamped postage was mailed from this former post office on May 2nd, 1840. The stamps, which later came to be known as "Penny Blacks," weren't scheduled to go into circulation until May 6, 1840, but this provincial post office got the date wrong, and is now part of postal history. Tour the museum, which chronicles the origin and use of stamps from their relatively recent beginnings to the current day. The museum is open Monday through Saturday from 11am to 5pm, Sunday from 2 to 5pm. There is a small admission charge.

Exit the museum, turn right onto Broad Street, then right again, onto Green Street. At the end of Green Street, turn left onto Old Bond Street. Turn right onto Upper Borough Walls to the:

18. Royal Mineral Water Hospital, a medical clinic established in 1742 for the purpose of using Bath's curative waters to combat diseases. In the 18th and 19th centuries, admitted patients were required to present a certificate of recommendation from their parish churches, and deposit £3 with the hospital bursar. The fee was used to pay for the patient's transport home after the cure—otherwise for the burial.

Walk through the iron gate located opposite the hospital, go down the steps, and look at the remains of the:

19. **City Wall,** a medieval protective wall built on top of older Roman-era foundations. The ground on which you are now standing was once the burial ground for patients who died at the Royal Mineral Water Hospital. The cemetery was closed in 1849, after receiving 238 bodies.

Walk back up the stairs and turn left onto Trim Street, which curves left. A half a block ahead, on your right, is the former:

20. **Home of General James Wolfe.** A manic depressive who moved to Bath for health reasons, Wolfe (1727–1759) later commanded the English forces that fought the French for Québec, Canada. Renowned as a fine leader and a brilliant military tactician, Wolfe took the French by surprise and captured Québec in a remarkable battle that lasted all of 11 minutes. But the fight cost the general his life. Wounded and dying, he was carried back behind the lines. When he was told of his victory he said, "Now God be praised, I will die in peace."

Turn right, under the arch located just past Wolfe's home, and walk straight on Queen Street to:

21. **Harington's Restaurant,** located on your left. The restaurant is named for the Haringtons, a family that once owned this land. The landowner's ancestor, Sir John Harington, was not only the favorite godson of Queen Elizabeth I, he is credited with the invention of the water closet—the first indoor toilet. Although no one can be sure, it is probable that the W.C.'s nickname "john" is derived from the room's inventor.

Notice that some of the windows of this building have been bricked up. In 1782 a tax was levied on all buildings according to the number of windows they had. To reduce the tax, many owners throughout the country bricked-up the less important windows of their houses—an example of which you can see here.

Walk another block along Queen Street to the intersection of John, Wood, and Quiet streets. These streets were designed by local architect John Wood, who was anxious for the Bath city council to name his completed streets. The council stalled and Wood nagged and cajoled, argued and threatened. The developer attended meeting after meeting, and was so persistent and vociferous in demanding a decision that the council chairman snapped "Quiet John Wood." The architect left the meeting smiling and named these streets "Quiet," "John," and "Wood."

Our walk ends at this intersection. From here you can either turn left onto Wood Street and begin Walking Tour 6, which commences at Queen Square;   or turn left onto Wood Street and make your way back to Bath Abbey via Barton Street and Westgate Street.

WALKING TOUR 6

Bath Part II

Start: The intersection of Barton Street and Queen Square.
Finish: The Roman Baths and Museum, Abbey Churchyard.
Time: 2 hours, not including rest stops.
Best Times: Daily between 9am and 5pm.
Worst Times: Early morning and early evening, when many of the major sights are closed.

For almost four centuries Bath's Roman ruins lay covered in mud, which helped to preserve them. Eventually they were built over and lost to sight. The hot spring, of course, continued its flow, and people came to bathe in its curative waters. The King's Bath was built in the 12th century, and by the 16th century three baths were in use.

Bath's renaissance began when Princess Anne visited the waters in 1702. By the late 18th century, Bath had been popularized into a fad by the flamboyant Beau Nash, who ruled Bath society as the arbiter of taste and manners. As construction of new baths and buildings went on during this period, Roman artifacts began to come to light, and Roman structures began to be accidentally uncovered.

But it was not until the 1880s that real excavations began, revealing what we see of the baths today. Much remains covered, however, and there are many discoveries still to be made.

Start at the intersection of Barton Street and:

1. **Queen Square,** one of the first urban squares in Britain. If you tour London and other English cities, you will notice that squares abound—London's Trafalgar Square is one of the most famous. But it was this square, in Bath, built in 1732 by architect John Wood, that revolutionized urban development. Queen Square was the country's first planned square, sketched out before it was built, with a palace on the north side and flanked by lesser buildings on the three other sides. In his project notes, architect Wood wrote "the intention of a square in a city is for people to assemble together; and the spot whereon they meet ought to be separated from the ground common to men and Beasts, and even to Mankind in general, if decency and good order are to be observed. . . ."

   Walk clockwise around the square, pausing at:

2. **Jane Austen's Lodgings,** 13 Queen Square, on your left. Novelist Jane Austen lodged here with her family for about six weeks during the summer of 1799. The young writer immediately sat down to record her first impressions of the house: "Well, here we are at Bath; we got here about one o'clock, and have been arrived just long enough to go over the house, fix on our rooms and be very well pleased with the whole of it . . . we are exceedingly pleased with the house; the rooms are quite as large as expected. Mrs. Bromley (the landlady) is a fat woman in mourning, and a little black kitten runs about the staircase . . ." Later, Jane made use of her experiences in Bath in her novel, *Northanger Abbey*.

   Continue around the square, stopping at the plaque marking the site of the former:

3. **Home of Dr. William Oliver,** one of Bath's most celebrated physicians. Oliver (1695–1764) helped found the Royal Mineral Water Hospital (see Stop 18 in "Walking Tour 5") and was the medical center's chief doctor for 21 years. It was there that Oliver came to the conclusion that many of the physical ills known to humankind are the result of overeating. As a remedy, Oliver invented the first digestive biscuit, a simple flour-water-and-sugar cookie that is still today a staple English snack.

   Walk further around the square to the former:

4. **Home of John Wood,** the elder, 24 Queen Square. One of Bath's chief architects, John Wood (1704–1754) left school at the age of 12 to become an apprentice joiner for his father, a local builder. Upon completion of his apprenticeship, Wood left

BATH PART II

N 0 ▭▭▭ 200 m
          220 y

Crescent Ln.
Julian Rd.
Guinea Ln.
Guinea Ln.
Walcot St.
Crescent Ln.
Royal Crescent
12
11
Royal Victoria Park
10
9
Brock St.
Bennett St.
Lansdown Rd.
Paragon St.
6
Alfred St.
7
8
Royal Ave.
Gravel Walk
Bartlett St.
Crescent Gardens
Gay St.
George St.
Old King St.
4
5
Milsom St.
Broad St.
Northgate St.
River Avon
St. John's Rd.
Bristol Rd.
Charlotte St.
3
1
2
start here
Barton St.
John St.
Quiet St.
Green St.
New Bond St.
Pulteney Bridge
Argyle St.
Grand Parade
Beaufort St.
Trim St.
Upper Borough Walls
Bridge St.
High St.
Charles St.
Monmouth St.
13
14
Sawclose
Union St.
Union Passage
Cheap St.
Orange Grove
Parade Gardens
James St. West
Westgate St.
19
finish here
York St.
Church St.
North Parade
Midland Bridge Rd.
Green Park Rd.
15 **18**
16
17
Bath St.
Stall St.
Henry St.
Pierrepont St.
Green Park
Avon St.
St. James Parade
Orchard St.
Southgate St.
Manvers St.
River Avon
Lower Bristol Rd.
Dorchester St.
Wells Rd.
Churchill Bridge
Claverton St.
Church

1. Queen Square
2. Jane Austen's Lodgings
3. Home of Dr. William Oliver
4. Home of John Wood, the elder
5. House of John Wood, the younger
6. Assembly Rooms
7. The Circus
8. Home of Major John Andre
9. Methodist Chapel of Bath
10. Royal Crescent

11. No. 1 Royal Crescent
12. Home of Sir Issac Pitman
13. Theatre Royal
14. The Garrick's Head
15. St. John's Hospital
16. Nowhere Place
17. Abbey Church House
18. Cross Bath
19. Roman Baths and Museum

6657

Bath to build fashionable houses in London and Yorkshire. In addition to being an architect, Wood wrote several books about Stonehenge and other megalithic monuments which he believed to be ancient astronomical temples. Strongly influenced by the ideas and works of the Italian neoclassical architect Palladio, Wood returned to Bath in 1727 and designed many of Bath's buildings using ancient Roman styles as inspirational models. Because Bath's developers were more interested in saving money than in architectural integrity, however, Wood was only contracted to create buildings' facades; his neoclassical interiors remained on the drawing boards.

Exit Queen Square via Gay Street (which was named after Dr. Gay, a former owner of the land on which this section of Bath was built) and pause outside the former:

5. House of John Wood, the younger, 41 Gay Street. The younger John (1728–1801) followed in his father's architectural footsteps, working on many buildings around Bath.

Look through the house's ground-floor window at the blue tiled room. This is an original "powder room," where 18th-century men and women once powdered their wigs.

Walk two more blocks along Gay Street, then turn right onto George Street. After about four blocks, cross over the pedestrian crossing. Go right, then turn left onto Bartlett Street. At the end of the street, turn left onto Alfred Street, walk to the end and turn right to arrive at:

6. The Assembly Rooms, an important meeting place for Bath society in the 18th century. Built by John Wood the younger at a cost of £20,000, the building was designed with four main rooms—a magnificent ballroom (the largest room in Bath at the time), The Octagon (a large meeting space), The Card Room, and The Tea Room.

In the 18th century, The Assembly was the most popular social soirée, often attended by over 1,000 revelers, and featured dancing, tea drinking, and card playing in the building's various rooms. By the beginning of the 19th century, regular concerts, recitals, and other entertainments took place in The Assembly Rooms. Composers Johann Strauss and Franz Liszt performed here, as did the famous dwarf General Tom Thumb, and even Charles Dickens came to give his public readings.

Continue along Bennett Street and walk into:

7. The Circus, a vehicular "roundabout" encircled by Roman-esque buildings. The Circus was the most innovative architectural work of the elder John Wood. The design was based on the Colosseum in Rome, turned inside out. Three different styles of classical architectural columns decorate the front of each house—Doric on the ground floor, Ionic on the second, and Corinthian on the third. The frieze that decorates the tops of the doorways depicts over 500 symbols of art, science, and nature: fruit, flowers, weapons, masonic signs, tragic masks, and many more.

Turn left onto The Circus and stop at the former:

8. Home of Major John Andre, 22 The Circus. Born and educated in Geneva, Switzerland, Andre (1751–1780) came to Bath with his family at age 19. A spy for England during the American War of Independence, Andre was accused of recruiting American traitor Benedict Arnold, and was hanged.

Backtrack, walking counterclockwise around The Circus where you will pass several notable former homes: artist Thomas Gainsborough (1727–1788) lived at no. 17; Lord Clive (1725–1774) lived at no. 14; and explorer David Livingstone (1813–1873) stayed in the basement of no. 13, after returning from Africa where he "discovered" the Zambezi River.

Exit The Circus via Brock Street and walk to the archway that stands about three blocks ahead on your right. Through this archway once stood:

9. The Methodist Chapel of Bath, a small church where the Methodist sect's co-founder, John Wesley, frequently preached. In one of these sermons, Wesley denounced the lifestyle of Beau Nash, Bath's most flamboyant socialite. Soon afterward, Wesley and Nash bumped into each other here on Brock Street. Nash blocked the sidewalk and said to Wesley, "I never give way to fools." Stepping off the pavement to make way for Nash, Wesley responded, "However, Mr. Nash, I do!"

Walk one block further along Brock Street to:

10. Royal Crescent, another beautiful architectural masterpiece created by the younger John Wood. Begun in 1767, the crescent contains 30 houses that, when built, stood on the very edge of the City of Bath. Wood's crescent idea was copied several times in Bath and became a popular architectural style in other English cities as well. The seminal Royal Crescent, however, is still regarded by critics as "the finest crescent in Europe."

As you enter Royal Crescent pause at:

11. No. 1 Royal Crescent, a home built for John Wood's father-in-law Thomas Brock, but today owned by the Bath Preservation Trust, a historical society that has restored the interior and furnished it in 18th-century style. The house is open to the public Tuesday through Sunday from 10:30am to 4pm. There is a small admission charge.

Exit the museum, turn right, and continue around the crescent to the former:

12. **Home of Sir Isaac Pitman,** 17 Royal Crescent. Pitman (1813–1897) invented what is now the most commonly used system of English-language shorthand. When Pitman arrived in Bath in 1839, he was moved to write: "Of the many beautiful cities in this fair country, Bath is unquestionably the most beautiful." The day before Pitman died—in this house, at age 84—he sent a brief note to his local clergyman in which he wrote, "To those who ask how Isaac Pitman died, say 'peacefully, and with no more concern than in passing from one room to another. . . .'"

Walk back to The Circus, turn right onto the roundabout, then exit The Circus onto Gay Street. Continue straight, onto Barton Street, then turn right onto Trim Street, to:

REFUELING STOP Popjoy's Restaurant, Trim Street (tel. 0225/447476). The restaurant is located in the former house of Juliana Popjoy, mistress of Beau Nash. Beau himself moved into this home after he relinquished his own grand house as part of a gambling debt owed to his friend, actor David Garrick. When one puritan admonished Nash for keeping a mistress, the socialite replied, "A man can no more be termed a whoremonger for having one whore in his house than a cheesemonger for having one cheese!" Nash died here in 1761, an event that so distressed Popjoy that the mistress vowed she would never again sleep in the bed they had shared. Popjoy returned to her native Wiltshire where she became a recognized local eccentric, living in a hollow tree until she died 17 years later.

The building adjacent to Popjoy's Restaurant, on Sawclose, is:

13. **The Theatre Royal,** Sawclose Street, one of Bath's most illustrious stages. Not surprisingly, some of the world's greatest actors performed here, including Sarah Bernhardt, Sir Henry Irving, and Ellen Terry. What many people do not know is that one of the world's worst actors was here too. Robert "Romeo" Coates (1772–1842), West Indies–born son of a wealthy American sugar plantation owner, became interested in dramatics as a young boy. When he inherited his father's estate, at age 35, the would-be actor headed for England to make a career. Despite abundant criticism—which Coates reasoned was the result of

jealousy—the wealthy actor was convinced of his own talent. Coates arrived in Bath in 1807 riding in a diamond-encrusted, shell-shaped carriage adorned with a gilded cockerel bearing his family motto, "While I live, I'll crow." While reciting Shakespeare in public places around town, Coates often altered the playwright's soliloquies, then observed, "I fancy that is rather better." Coates' unabashed egotism soon brought the young sugar-cane heir to the attention of the manager of the Theatre Royal, who contracted Coates for a single evening to play the role of Romeo in Shakespeare's *Romeo and Juliet*. The show sold out. When Coates appeared on stage, the mocking audience broke into ecstatic cheers, and the actor stopped to acknowledge them! The Romeo that Shakespeare described as a "quiet, virtuous and well-governed youth" appeared that night in bright crimson pantaloons, a spangled, sky-blue coat, and a white feathered hat sparkling with diamonds. Throughout the play, audience members hurled orange peels onto the stage while crowing "cock-a-doodle-do." To the "fans" delight, Coates would halt—mid-sentence—and crow back at them. As the play drew to a close and Shakespeare's immortal lovers were about to be reunited in death, Romeo appeared on stage with a crow bar and, diverging from Shakespeare's script, began to pry open Juliet's tomb. The audience booed and jeered, Coates returned their insults, and the distraught theater manager brought the curtain down. An unmitigated success, Coates went on to tour the British Isles, delighting audiences wherever he went.

Continue along Sawclose to the pub called:

14. The Garrick's Head. This was the former home of Richard "Beau" Nash. The son of a wealthy glass manufacturer, Nash attended Oxford University but left without obtaining a degree. Richard's father bought him a commission in the army, but military discipline didn't agree with him either. Nash attempted law school, but failed there as well. Eventually, Richard became a professional gambler, and his extravagant clothing and ostentatious lifestyle earned him the nickname "Beau."

Soon after he came to Bath, in order to pursue his chosen career, Beau became the assistant to Bath's master of ceremonies—a semiofficial social director. When the master of ceremonies was killed in a duel, Nash assumed the unpaid post, and immediately set about transforming Bath's social scene. To this end, he ensured the city's streets were regularly cleaned, licensed taxis, imposed codes of dress and behavior, and banned dueling. Nash flattered England's aristocrats with his courtly manners; his reforms raised the town's quality and stature, and attracted the money that was used to build the magnificent public buildings you see today.

For more than 50 years Nash was widely known as "the King of Bath," and earned most of his money from the city's casino profits. When England's moral attitudes turned against casinos, Nash's income dried up, and the King of Bath died relatively poor.

Continue along Sawclose, which runs into Westgate Buildings. After about five short blocks turn left through the iron gates of:

15. St. John's Hospital. Founded in 1174 from public donations, the hospital has the distinction of being the oldest charity in Bath. The buildings are now almshouses. St. John's still continues giving one or two of its residents one pound a week after attending services each Thursday to keep an old tradition alive.

Retrace your footsteps to Westgate Buildings and pause at the small garden on your right that's popularly known as:

16. Nowhere Place. The garden got its name because maids from Abbey House used to come here to cavort with the local lads. Caught sneaking back into the house and quizzed as to where they had been, they often replied, "Nowhere!" So the garden became known as Nowhere Place.

Turn right, down the passageway located just past the garden. The building on your right is:

17. Abbey Church House. This 1570 structure earns mention here because it is typical of the 16th-century construction that was typical of the city before Bath's intensive rebuilding in the 18th century.

At the end of the passageway turn left, and walk to the fence that surrounds:

18. Cross Bath, an 800-year-old bathing pool favored by 18th-century nobility. Queen Mary of Modena, wife of King James II, brought fame to this bath after a dip here successfully cured her of infertility.

Take a look at the exceptionally small house opposite the bath and examine the 14th-century statue in the left-hand niche on the house's facade. The sculpture is of 10th-century King Edgar, who was crowned in Bath Abbey in A.D. 973. A contemporary scribe recorded the event in some detail. Since the coronation ceremony had little precedence to draw upon, coronation rituals had to be invented; several of these ceremonial features persist to this day.

Return to Cross Bath and continue walking straight, onto Bath Street. Turn left onto Stall Street, then right into Abbey Churchyard. At the end of the yard, turn right, and enter:

19. The Roman Baths and Museum, Abbey Churchyard (tel. 0225/461111). The site of the 1st-century temple to the Celtic water goddess Sul and the Roman goddess Minerva, this natural spring was the foundation of the original town of Bath. Although almost every Roman town had both temples and baths, Aquae Sulis or "Sul's Spa" as it was known in Roman times, became famous for its special curative powers. The structures that were built to house the spring were some of the finest in Roman Britain.

To enter the baths, visitors pass through a museum that traces the area's history from Roman times to the current day. Contemporary excavations have unearthed many historical objects, including jewelry and other personal effects. Some may have fallen off accidentally, others were tossed into the waters as offerings to the goddesses.

After touring the baths, exit into the:

FINAL REFUELING STOP **Pump Room and Restaurant,** Abbey Churchyard (tel. 0225/444477). Along with a wide variety of traditional English-style foods, visitors have the opportunity to do what people have been doing here for almost 2,000 years—drink the waters. And what do they taste like? In Charles Dickens's novel *The Pickwick Papers,* John Smauker asks his companion Sam Weller what he thinks of Bath's waters, as the two stroll along High Street. "I thought they was particklerly unpleasant," Sam replied. "Ah" said Mr. John Smauker, "you disliked the killibeate taste, perhaps?" "I don't know much about that 'ere" said Sam, "I thought they'd a very strong flavour o'warm flat irons." "That IS the killibeate, Mr. Weller" was the reply.

Stratford-upon-Avon

Start: Shakespeare's Birthplace, Henley Street.
Finish: Tourist Information Center, Bridgefoot.
Time: About 2 hours, not including rest stops.
Best Times: Daily from 9am to 5:30pm (during winter months from 10am to 4pm), when most of the sights are open.
Worst Times: Early mornings and late evenings, when most of the sights on this tour are closed.

Stratford-upon-Avon—often just called Stratford—is named for the river it straddles, the Avon, which is Welsh for "river." A beautiful market town with its picture-perfect half-timbered houses, it would probably attract sightseers even without its famous son, William Shakespeare. Born here in April 1564, Shakespeare grew up, was married, and then left Stratford around 1590 to pursue fame and fortune in London. He returned to his hometown less than 10 years later, a rich and famous man.

Ever since the first Shakespeare festival was held in 1769, most of the town's prosperity has come from its Shakespearean connections and today Stratford-upon-Avon is the most visited tourist town in England after London. Thousands of people arrive here daily and the first thing you will notice is just how crowded the place is. Hordes of tourists stream through its small streets, focusing their attentions mainly on the birthplace.

Don't be put off. Our route will keep you well out of the way of crowds most of the time, though you will encounter them at the birthplace and around the theaters. Other than that, you're in for a delightful leisurely stroll through a magical little town.

When you have finished our stroll, if you are still up for a walk, you can take a very pleasant and well-marked walk to Shottery and Anne Hathaway's cottage, through fields, lanes, and footpaths.

MONEY-SAVING TIP: Our walk visits three of five properties administered by the Shakespeare Trust. If, before or after this walk, you intend to do some additional touring, it is most economical to purchase an inclusive five-property ticket. If you intend only to visit the three properties included on this walk, you will save money by paying for each entrance individually.

Our walk begins, appropriately enough, at:

1. **Shakespeare's Birthplace** (tel. 0789/204016), on Henley Street, half a block north of the post office. William Shakespeare was born in this house in 1564. His father was John Shakespeare, a glover and whittawer (skin-and-wool dealer). His mother, Mary Arden, came from the landowning gentry; her father, Robert Arden, was the head of a minor branch of an old Warwickshire family. Shakespeare's grandfather, Richard Shakespeare, had lived in the village of Snitterfield, about 3 miles north of Stratford, and had farmed land on the manor belonging to Mary's family. Mary must have been a good match for John, to whom she brought higher social standing as well as properties in the nearby village of Wilmcote.

An ambitious man, John embarked on the first rung of the local government ladder when he was appointed the town aletaster in 1556, an office designed to ensure that brewers sold wholesome beer and bakers made full-weight bread. In 1558 he progressed to parish constable.

Two daughters were born before William, but both died in infancy, possibly victims of a virulent outbreak in the midlands of bubonic plague. The plague abated in 1564, just a few months before the Shakespeares' third child was christened in the parish church of the Holy Trinity on April 26 as *Guilielmus filius Johannes Shakespere.*

William was born into a well-to-do middle-class family. John's ambitions had seen him rise to a town burgess, and in

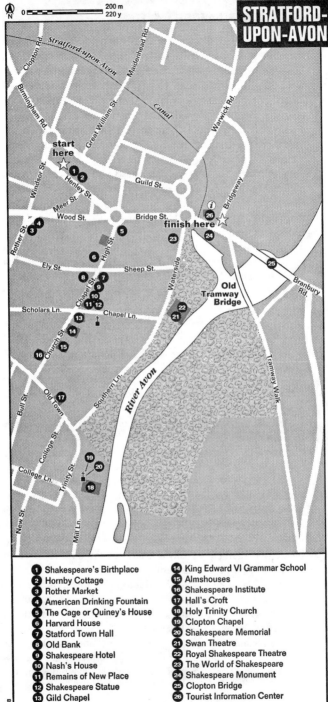

STRATFORD-UPON-AVON

0 ___ 200 m
___ 220 y

N

start here

Stratford-upon-Avon

Clopton Rd.
Birmingham Rd.
Maidenhead Rd.
Warwick Rd.
Great William St.
Canal
Guild St.
Bridgeway
Windsor St.
Henley St.
Meer St.
Wood St.
Bridge St.
finish here
Rother St.
High St.
Ely St.
Sheep St.
Waterside
Old Tramway Bridge
Branbury Rd.
Chapel St.
Scholars Ln.
Chapel Ln.
Church St.
Bull St.
Old Town
Southern Ln.
River Avon
Tramway Walk
College St.
New St.
Trinity St.
Mill Ln.
College Ln.

Church ✝ Information ℹ

1 Shakespeare's Birthplace
2 Hornby Cottage
3 Rother Market
4 American Drinking Fountain
5 The Cage or Quiney's House
6 Harvard House
7 Statford Town Hall
8 Old Bank
9 Shakespeare Hotel
10 Nash's House
11 Remains of New Place
12 Shakespeare Statue
13 Gild Chapel
14 King Edward VI Grammar School
15 Almshouses
16 Shakespeare Institute
17 Hall's Croft
18 Holy Trinity Church
19 Clopton Chapel
20 Shakespeare Memorial
21 Swan Theatre
22 Royal Shakespeare Theatre
23 The World of Shakespeare
24 Shakespeare Monument
25 Clopton Bridge
26 Tourist Information Center

6658

1569 he was elected town bailiff, the officer responsible for all the town's affairs. In 1571 he was appointed chief alderman. However he had apparently been neglecting his business, and when William was about 12 years old, financial difficulties caused him to withdraw from the council. Property had to be sold, and lawsuits followed.

Upon leaving school, William may have worked with his father. But before he was 18, he got involved with Anne Hathaway, a farmer's daughter from the nearby village of Shottery. Anne became pregnant, a hasty marriage was arranged, and on Sunday, May 26, 1583, their first child was christened Susanna in the parish church. Within two years Anne had also given birth to twins, a son, Hamnet, who died in childhood, and a daughter, Judith.

We do not know what caused William to leave Stratford and make his way to London. The fact is that at some stage, between 1585 and 1592, Shakespeare went to London, and within 10 years was able to return wealthy enough to rescue the family fortunes.

Over the years, Shakespeare's Birthplace has passed through a number of hands. By the 19th century, the house had become a museum dedicated to the famous playwright, and Mrs. Mary Hornby was the tenant of the house. However, when Washington Irving visited the house in 1815, he was not impressed by what he described as "a small mean-looking edifice of wood and plaster." His guide, Mrs. Mary Hornby, impressed him even less. He recalls with disdain that she showed him "Shakespeare's tobacco."

Mary Hornby made a good living by charging visitors to see her museum of "authentic" Shakespeare mementoes. Forced from the house after her landlord's death by his widow, who was envious of her little empire, Mrs. Hornby took her Shakespeare relics to cheaper lodgings across the street, and the widow opened her own museum. Competition between the two became intense—they would stand in their respective doorways and berate one another, verbally abusing any visitor who dared to enter the opposition's museum.

In 1847 the house was offered for sale as "the most honored monument of the greatest genius that ever lived." Committees were formed to raise money to buy it, and it was preserved as a national memorial to Shakespeare.

The birthplace is now restored to something approaching its original form. Rooms are furnished in period style, and you pass through John Shakespeare's shop with an exhibition of the house's history. Upstairs, the birth room is exhibited; there is no evidence to suggest this was actually where Shakespeare was born, but there is no evidence against it either. On the windows of the room can be seen the diamond-scratched signatures of Tennyson, Walter Scott, Thomas Carlyle, Washington Irving, Ellen Terry, and others.

Exit the birthplace into a delightful garden where, in the summer, all the flowers mentioned in the plays of Shakespeare explode into a profusion of yellows, reds, pinks, and purples. Don't hurry as so many visitors do—enjoy one of Stratford's loveliest attractions.

Exit the birthplace via the souvenir shop, located in:

2. Hornby Cottage, the house next door. Named for Richard Hornby, the blacksmith who worked here during Shakespeare's time, the cottage was purchased in 1902 by American philanthropist Andrew Carnegie, who, in turn, donated it to the Trustees of Shakespeare's Birthplace.

Exiting the cottage, turn right onto Henley Street, keeping to the left side of the street. Number 45 dates from the early 1600s; note the snarling dog with a crown on the top right gutter pipe. Take a left at the second alley, which leads into Minories Shopping Mall, lined with tasteful little craft shops.

At the end of the mall, turn right onto Meer Street, which leads into Rother Street. One block ahead on the right is the beautiful half-timbered White Swan Hotel. Continue along Rother Street to the pedestrian crossing, and cross the road to note the Old Thatched Tavern, whose license dates back to 1623. To the left of the Old Thatch, walk about three blocks to see Mason's Court, the best preserved 15th-century Tudor dwelling in Stratford. Cross the road for the best view, and note the overhanging roof of handmade tiles and the bowed chimney stacks.

Backtrack along Rother Street to:

3. Rother Market. The word "rother" derives from Old English *Hreothr,* which means "cattle," a word recalled by Shakespeare in *Timon of Athens:* "it is the pasture lards the rother's sides." Rother Market was Stratford's principal cattle market during Shakespeare's day.

On the far side of the market is the:

4. American Drinking Fountain, an 1887 gift to the city of Stratford. The inscription above the fountain, "Honest water which ne'er left man the mire" is from Shakespeare's *Timon of Athens.*

From the fountain, turn right onto Wood Street. The second building on your right is:

REFUELING STOP The Chapter and Verse Book Shop, Wood Street. This delightful old building sells second-hand books on the first floor, and the upstairs front room with its slanting floor is a tea shop, serving tea along with a selection of English cakes.

Exit and turn right onto Wood Street. Continue to the end and turn right onto High Street. The building to your immediate left is:

5. **The Cage or Quiney's House,** which once had a temporary lock-up for petty criminals attached to it. It was home to Shakespeare's youngest daughter, Judith, and her husband, wine merchant Thomas Quiney, from 1616 to 1637. Not long before the couple's marriage, Quiney got a young woman named Margaret Wheeler pregnant. She died while giving birth to the child, and Thomas was brought before the ecclesiastical court, commonly called "bawdy court" because it primarily heard cases of sexual offenses. He confessed and was sentenced to perform "open penance" in front of an entire church congregation on three successive Sundays, but bought off his sentence by paying 5 shillings to the poor of the parish. There is some evidence to suggest that the shock of the case and the subsequent scandal may have hastened the demise of his already ailing father-in-law, William Shakespeare, in April 1616.

   Continue walking along High Street, which is lined with several splendid timber-framed buildings. About three blocks ahead, on your right, is:

6. **Harvard House,** built by a butcher, Thomas Rogers. There is a local tradition that Shakespeare worked here for a short while as an apprentice butcher. Thomas Rogers was the grandfather of John Harvard, benefactor of the American college that became Harvard University and bears his name. The house was restored by Edward Morris, an American historian, and given to Harvard University in 1909.

   Next door to Harvard House is:

REFUELING STOP The Garrick Inn, High Street (tel. 292186). The building dates back to 1594. In 1718 it became an inn called the Reindeer, then the Greyhound, and briefly New Inn, The Garrick was renamed in 1769, after the famous Shakespearean actor David Garrick.

In addition to traditional, inexpensive "pub grub," served daily until 9pm, the tavern features a good variety of unusual beers, including Castle Eden and Flowers.

Exit the Garrick Inn and walk directly across High Street, onto Sheep Street. The building on your left is:

7. Stratford Town Hall. Look up at the three windows facing you to see the statue of Shakespeare in a niche above the middle window. When the hall was rebuilt in 1767, actor David Garrick was asked to provide a statue for the niche above the center window. Garrick commissioned artist John Cheere to make the sculpture—it's an exact copy of a statue of Shakespeare that stands in Westminster Abbey.

When the statue was put in place in 1769, Garrick organized the world's first Shakespearean festival, supposedly to celebrate the bicentenary of Shakespeare's birth—the egotistical Garrick was not deterred by the fact that his date was five years too late or in the wrong month. It was not altogether a success. At 6am on September 6, guns boomed out to announce that the festival had begun, but on the second day it rained so heavily that the great pageant of Shakespearean characters had to be cancelled. Fireworks and a fancy dress ball were planned, but as the actress Mrs. Baddeley sang "Soft thou gently flowing Avon," the river burst its banks, soaked the fireworks, and marooned the dancers, who made it to dry land with difficulty. The festival had to be abandoned, and was concluded with only one line of the Bard's being quoted, and that incorrectly.

Town Hall is rarely open to the public, but is worth a look inside if it is. Walk through the building's front doors and ring the small bell on your left, marked "Ring Custodian," who will tell you whether or not you can look around. Inside the council chamber is a historical list of Stratford's bailiffs and other administrative officials, including, of course, William Shakespeare's father, John. In the ballroom is a portrait of Garrick as Richard III.

Exit Town Hall, turn left onto Sheep Street, and return to the High Street intersection. Turn left onto Chapel Street where you'll see the:

8. Old Bank, a treasury and lending society established in 1810.

The paintings adorning the bank's red brick walls depict scenes from several of Shakespeare's plays. A few doors down is:

9. **The Shakespeare Hotel,** which is located in the former home of a wealthy citizen of Stratford. The hotel, which was originally called The Four Gables, was sold in 1782 to innkeeper John Nickals, who renamed the hostel "The Shakespeare's Head," giving this business the distinction of being the first in Stratford to exploit the Bard's name.

A few steps farther along Chapel Street you'll see:

10. **Nash's House,** the former home of Shakespeare's grand-daughter, Elizabeth Hall, and her husband, Thomas Nash. Nash died in 1647, after 21 years of marriage, and the widowed Elizabeth took a second husband, John Bernard of Northamptonshire. In November, 1661, King Charles II granted Bernard a baronetcy in return for his services to the state during the English Civil War. Shakespeare's granddaughter Elizabeth became Lady Bernard, and the Shakespeare family joined the aristocracy. The Shakespeare family's noble status was to be short-lived, however. When Lady Bernard died childless in 1670, direct descendants of William Shakespeare—both male and female—became extinct.

Tour this house, which contains fine examples of Tudor- and Jacobean-style furnishings, along with a fascinating museum tracing the history of Stratford-upon-Avon.

Exit Nash House through the rear gardens to the:

11. **Remains of New Place,** the grand Stratford home that Shakespeare purchased after gaining fame in London. By 1597 his considerable success in London meant he was able to afford a magnificent home in Stratford for his family. When Shakespeare bought it for £50, the home was a bona fide fixer-upper. We can imagine the playwright delighting in the purchase of his first house, setting about rebuilding it, and settling down with his wife and two young daughters. *Henry IV,* which was written around this time, is full of images that show his preoccupation with property renovation.

The house eventually passed to Shakespeare's daughter, Susanna, and tradition has it that during the English Civil War in 1643 Queen Henrietta Maria, wife of Charles 1, came to stay with Susanna at New Place.

New Place changed hands a number of times, finally being purchased by Reverend George Gastrell, a wealthy but cantankerous clergyman who detested the constant stream of tourists who flocked here, especially to see a mulberry tree in the garden supposedly planted by Shakespeare. He chopped down the tree, and after a protracted argument with the local government about property taxes, demolished the house as an act of defiance, but was forced to leave town "amidst the rage and curses of the inhabitants." The only thing remaining of New Place today are some foundations in the garden along with two water wells.

Leave the garden through the opening in the hedge to see the Knott Garden, a delightful reconstruction of a formal Elizabethan garden, with an intricate pattern of flowerbeds edged by miniature hedges.

Exit this area via a wooden turnstile, and follow the gravel pathway to the left to the:

12. **Shakespeare Statue,** a blackened sculpture depicting the seated playwright between the muses of drama and painting. The statue's soiled state is a result of formerly being positioned on Pall Mall, in central London. The statue was relocated here in 1871.

Exit the garden and turn right onto Chapel Lane. At the end of the lane, on your left, is:

13. **Gild Chapel,** a church founded in 1269 by the Gild of the Holy Cross, a religious fraternity whose sole purpose was to ensure the salvation of its members. Membership in the fraternity was open to anyone who could afford its entrance fees, and payments were often met with donations of land. As a result, The Gild eventually became one of Stratford's most prominent owners of real estate.

The Gild was suppressed in 1553 during the Reformation; the chapel and The Gild's lands were confiscated by the king and granted to the newly formed Council of Stratford. They are still owned by the city today.

Exit Gild Chapel and turn left onto Chapel Street, which soon changes its name to Church Street. Just ahead, on your left, is:

14. **King Edward VI Grammar School,** Church Street, a still functioning grade school established in 1427 by the Gild of the Holy Cross for the purpose of educating the sons of the members. After The Gild's properties were confiscated by the state in the 16th century, this building was turned over to the government, where it doubled as the headquarters of Stratford's new borough government.

In Shakespeare's youth, traveling companies of actors often performed here. They are first recorded during John Shakespeare's term as bailiff, when the Queen's Players were paid the sum of 9 shillings while performing here, but the Earl of

Worcester's Men failed to impress and were paid only 1 shilling. It is fitting that John Shakespeare should emerge as Stratford's first theatrical patron, though he could not have realized the destiny of his eldest son, then aged 5.

Since registers of the day have been destroyed, we cannot prove conclusively that William Shakespeare attended this school, but it seems likely that he did. Shakespeare certainly received some form of education, and his father was involved in this school's administration. It is fairly safe to assume that this was indeed where William went to school.

During Shakespeare's time, education began at the age of 4 or 5, not in grammar school, but in an attached "petty" school. The teacher here would have been an usher, sparing the master from what the town council described as "that tedious trouble of teaching the troublesome youth of the town." Those "troublesome youth" came to class equipped with a "horn-book," a leaf of parchment on which was written the alphabet and the Lord's Prayer framed in wood and covered with protective transparent horn. The mark of the cross preceded the alphabet, which was called the "Christ cross row." In *Richard III,* the duke of Clarence, arrested by his brother, Edward IV, and soon to be murdered, says of Edward:

> *He harkens after prophecies and dreams,*
> *And from the cross-row plucks the letter G*
> *And says a wizard told him that by G*
> *His issue disinherited should be;*
> *And, for my name of George begins with G*
> *It follows in his thought that I am he.*

From the petty school, the boys progressed to the grammar school, and Shakespeare in *The Merry Wives of Windsor* supposedly parodies his former master, Thomas Jenkins, as Sir Hugh Evans.

Unfortunately, the old school building is closed to the public. The building contains two small libraries, and a large upstairs room where most of the teaching takes place.

Next door to the grammar school are:

15. Almshouses. Built in 1427, these are probably the oldest extant domestic dwellings in Stratford and their appearance has changed little since Shakespeare's day. They were built by the Gild of the Holy Cross to house elderly people in need—a function they still perform today.

One block farther along Church Street, on your right, is a building with a large flag outside. This is the:

16. **Shakespeare Institute of the University of Birmingham,** a school focusing on Elizabethan studies. Built in 1725, the house was once the home of Queen Victoria's favorite novelist, Marie Corelli, who lived here from 1901 to 1924. The author of many bestsellers, Corelli was a noted eccentric who attracted the ire of her neighbors. She perpetually accused one next door neighbor of spying over their shared fence, sued a local newspaper for libel, and hired an authentic Venetian gondolier to ferry her up and down the River Avon. In 1907 Corelli achieved her greatest social coup by persuading author Mark Twain to visit this house in Stratford. Twain later confided that he had found the English authoress an "offensive sham."

Walk to the end of Church Street and turn left, onto the street called Old Town. The building halfway down on your left is:

17. **Hall's Croft,** the former home of Shakespeare's daughter, Susanna, and her husband, Dr. John Hall. The couple married in June 1607, when the young doctor was first starting to make a name for himself. The Halls bought this half-timbered house, and enlarged it to include an impressive consulting room and dispensary.

Dr. Hall treated a whole gamut of human ills with medicines distilled from roosters' guts, spider webs, and other non-traditional ingredients. He successfully treated scurvy with a special beer that was rich in ascorbic acid and diligently recorded his efforts in a medical diary that was published posthumously, in 1657, and called *Select Observations on English Bodies*. The diary records patients' cases in vivid detail. The Countess of Northhampton's chambermaid fell ill when her "arse-gut fell out," John Emes of Alcester was prone to "pissing in bed," and wife Susanna was administered an enema after complaining of being "miserably tormented with colic." According to records, the treatment "presently brought forth a great deal of wind, and freed her from all pain."

Visit this house, which is filled with period furniture and has a small but fascinating exhibition dedicated to the life and times of Dr. John Hall.

When Shakespeare made his will, he seems to have placed his trust largely in the competence and goodwill of his daughter and her husband. His will, written in January 1616 and revised in March after the Quiney scandal, is verified at the bottom of each page with the words "By me" and his signature. The three signatures are written with difficulty, suggesting that he must have been very ill at the time. He left the Halls the bulk of his property, obviously with the expectation that they were to look after his widow. The often quoted clause in the will, leaving his wife, Anne, their second-best bed, probably indicates that she was to keep her marriage bed, a special and thoughtful bequest.

REFUELING STOP The Restaurant at Hall's Croft, Old Town. This small eatery serves English pastries and pies in an unusually charming setting. It's open daily from 10am to 4pm.

Exit Hall's Croft and turn left onto Old Town. Walk past the three 16th-century buildings—Old Town Croft, Avon Croft, and The Dower House—and continue along the delightful lime-tree-lined pathway that turns into Trinity Street to:

18. Holy Trinity Church, one of England's stateliest medieval churches. The trees that line the approach to the church were planted symbolically; the 12 on the left side represent the tribes of Israel, and the 11 on the right symbolize the Apostles (minus Judas Iscariot).

The porch through which you enter dates from the 15th century, while the inner doors date from the 14th century. Note on the inner door the Sanctuary Knocker. This is a 13th-century sanctuary ring—any lawbreaker who reached it was allowed to claim sanctuary, or protection from the law for 37 days.

Enter the church's unusually low door, into the 14th-century nave, the main body of the church. Walk to the font and look down the aisle to notice how the chancel twists to the north. Known as a "weeping chancel," it was built to symbolize either Christ's head on the cross or else to make it more difficult for the devil to find the altar.

At the top of the north aisle, located to your left, is:

19. The Clopton Chapel, named for statesman and ambassador William Clopton. His effigy-topped tomb is located to your left. At age 19 Clopton served as a soldier in Ireland. He later became a naval commander, then ambassador to France, and finally a councillor of the American colony of Virginia. Clopton's tomb, carved by Edward Marshall, master mason to Charles II, has been called "the grandest Corinthian monuments in England."

A local legend about the Clopton family may have suggested to Shakespeare the idea for Juliet's awakening in the family vault to find her Romeo dead. We are told that Charlotte Clopton succumbed to the plague in 1564, and was buried in the family vault. Less than a week later, another member of the family died and was carried to the same vault. According to legend, when the tomb was opened for the second body, the horrified pall-bearers discovered Charlotte in a long white shroud leaning against the wall at the bottom of the steps. Apparently she had regained consciousness after being buried, then died of suffocation in the airless tomb.

Enter the church's chancel, for which a small fee is charged. Continue to the first altar to the left; you cannot enter, but you can admire the 15th-century vestry screen which was originally across the entry to the chancel. Opposite, in the south transept, is the magnificent "American Window," a gift from the U.S. ambassador in 1896.

Notice the misericords, the narrow ledges on the undersides of the hinged seats, designed to support elderly or infirm congregants who could not stand for long periods. Their woodcarvers were allowed considerable artistic freedom: Demons, birds, beasts, "wild men" are depicted, and one located near the priest's door shows a woman seizing a man by his beard while she beats him about the head with a pan.

Walk past the misericords and to the left you will see records from the church register certifying both the baptism and burial of William Shakespeare. Just past this is a 15th-century font in which baby Shakespeare was probably baptized, adjacent to a wall monument known as the:

20. Shakespeare Memorial. Erected shortly after Shakespeare's death in 1616, the bust depicts the bard looking like a well-lunched executive, holding a feather quill. The sculpture's face may have been modeled from the playwright's death mask, reflecting the body's bloated state just after death. Between the pair of cherubs on the cornice above the statue is the Shakespeare family's coat of arms.

John Shakespeare had applied to London's College of Arms for a family shield when he became bailiff of Stratford, but his financial problems caused him to withdraw the application. In 1596, William renewed the application and it was granted on the basis that Shakespeare's ancestors had valiantly assisted Henry VII at the Battle of Bosworth in 1485, and the shield carries the motto "Non Sans Droit," Latin for "Not Without Right." Shakespeare's contemporary, and professional rival, Ben Jonson, mocked his colleague's pretension to a family coat of arms in his play *Every Man in His Humour.* In Jonson's comedy, Sogliardo, a provincial clown, pays an absurdly high price for a coat of arms that carries the motto "Not Without Mustard."

Shakespeare is buried under the floor beneath the bust. An inscription on the grave reads:

> Good friend for Jesus' sake forbeare
> To digge the dust enclosed heare!
> Blest be ye man yt spares these stones
> And cursed be he yt moves my bones.

This curse, that's said to have been written by Shakespeare himself, was intended to discourage the church sexton from the common practice of removing the bones from the chancel and placing them in the charnel house so that the grave space might be used again.

Exit Holy Trinity Church and take a few minutes to explore the beautiful churchyard. Retrace your steps up Trinity Street, then turn right onto Southern Lane. Walk past **The Other Place** (tel. 078/929-5623), an experimental theater located on your left, and continue straight, as the street changes its name to Waterside. About three blocks ahead on your left is:

REFUELING STOP **The Black Swan,** Waterside (tel. 0789/297312). Although this pub's real name is The Black Swan, it is known locally as the Dirty Duck. The traditional haunt of actors from the nearby Royal Shakespeare Company, the bar is filled with signed "head shots," photographs that include many world-famous actors and actresses.

In addition to a selection of traditional "pub grub," the pub serves Tetley, Buton, and Wadsworths 6X beers.

Exit the Dirty Duck, turn left, and continue one block along Waterside to:

21. The Swan Theatre, Waterside (tel. 0789/29-6655), which stands on the site of the first Shakespeare Memorial Theatre, which opened in 1879. The Victorian Gothic-style building was inaugurated with a performance of Shakespeare's play *Much Ado About Nothing*. The first season was limited to a week's festival with such "star" visitors as Ellen Terry appearing in chosen roles. Under the direction of F. R. Benson, this grew to a two-month summer season. In 1925 a royal charter was granted, but only a year later the theater was almost totally destroyed by fire. The present structure is the result of a successful world-wide fundraising campaign to build a new theater. Today the Swan is home to the Royal Shakespeare Exhibition, a small museum dedicated to the life of Stratford's most famous resident.

The Swan is open April through October, Monday through Saturday from 9:15am to 8pm, and Sunday from noon to 5pm; November through March, daily from 11am to 4pm. Organized theater tours, lasting 45 minutes each, are scheduled year-round, Monday through Saturday at 1:30 and 5:30pm, and Sunday at 12:30, 1:30, 2:30, and 3:30pm.

Exit the Swan Theatre, turn right and walk about half a block to:

22. **The Royal Shakespeare Theatre,** home to the Royal Shakespeare Company (RSC), one of the best known theater troupes in the world. Performing regularly in both Stratford and London, RSC productions are attended by over one million theater-goers annually. The company traces its roots to 1875, when local brewer Charles Edward Flower donated 10 acres of land and launched a national campaign to build a theater in Stratford dedicated to the works of William Shakespeare. The actual building of the theater stalled, however, and was only realized in 1932, after the nearby Memorial Theatre burned down.

The RSC emerged as the foremost Shakespearean company in the 1940s, owing its success to artistic director Barry Jackson whose slogan was "productions before profits." Different directors and designers were brought in for each play, and the young talent that was fervently nurtured included actor Paul Scofield. The company continued to grow under Anthony Quayle, who brought established actors and "stars" to Stratford while still encouraging new talent: Michael Redgrave, Ralph Richardson, John Gielgud, Peggy Ashcroft, Vivien Leigh, and Laurence Olivier acted alongside talented unknowns like the young Richard Burton. Tours of Europe, Russia, and the United States plus invitations to actors and directors from abroad further widened the company's fame.

The Royal Shakespeare Company's commitment to touring has always been an integral part of its philosophy. In recent years the large-scale production of *Nicholas Nickleby* was a great success in America, *Richard III* has toured Australia, and *Les Liaisons Dangereuses* and *The Comedy of Errors* have visited Europe and Asia.

Walk along Waterside, about two blocks past the Royal Shakespeare Theatre, to:

23. **The World of Shakespeare,** an interesting audiovisual show that not only depicts the playwright's life, but re-creates scenes

of 16th-century Stratford. Shows are scheduled daily, every 30 minutes or so, continuously from 9:30am to 5pm. There is an admission charge.

Continue about one block along Waterside and turn right, onto Bridgefoot. Walk about one block, turn right into Bancroft Gardens, and pause at the:

24. **Shakespeare Monument,** a 65-ton bronze statue of a seated Shakespeare. Cast in Paris, the sculpture was a gift to the town of Stratford in 1888 by Lord Ronald Sutherland Gower. Originally installed behind Shakespeare Memorial Theatre, the statue was unveiled in a ceremony that included speeches by the eminent Victorian actor, George Augustus Sala, and dramatist Oscar Wilde. Several other statues—each depicting a character from one of Shakespeare's plays—stand adjacent to the monument. The sculpture immediately to the left of the memorial is Falstaff. Lady Macbeth is depicted sleepwalking, along with Macbeth's words, "Life's but a walking shadow, a poor player that struts and frets his hour upon the stage and then is heard no more." A statue of Hamlet holding Yorick's skull is inscribed with Horatio's farewell words, "Goodnight sweet prince and flights of angels sing thee to thy rest." Lastly, Prince Hal is depicted holding his crown aloft.

Exit Bancroft Gardens, turn right onto Bridgefoot, then bear right onto the pedestrian pathway. Continue straight, onto Old Tramway Bridge which crosses the River Avon, and look to your left, at:

25. **Clopton Bridge,** a 14-arched span donated to the Town of Stratford by Sir Hugh Clopton in the 14th century. The bridge brought with it renewed prosperity to the town. The bridge still functions as the main point of entry for travelers from London, and Shakespeare undoubtedly crossed it many times. When the span was repaired in the 16th century, much of the rebuilding was done with surplus stone from New Place, which Shakespeare purchased later.

Continue across Old Tramway Bridge to the other side of the river and turn left, onto the pathway that leads towards the river. The Swan's Nest Hotel, on your right, dates from the late 17th century, and was one of the first buildings in Stratford to be built of brick.

Turn left and recross the River Avon over Clopton Bridge. The small tower on the bridge's far left side dates from 1814 and once functioned as a toll house—a reminder of the days when travelers were routinely taxed for the use of municipal bridges.

Our tour ends on the far side of Clopton Bridge, at Stratford's:

26. **Tourist Information Center,** Bridgefoot (tel. 0789/29-3127). This helpful tourist office offers information, advice, and a helpful accommodations-booking service. It's open April through October, Monday through Saturday from 9am to 5:30pm, Sunday from 2 to 5pm; November through March, Monday through Saturday from 10:30am to 4:30pm (closed Sunday).

WALKING TOUR 8

Chester

Start: The Cross, at the intersection of Northgate, Eastgate, Watergate, and Bridge streets.
Finish: The Cross, at the intersection of Northgate, Eastgate, Watergate, and Bridge streets.
Time: 2 hours, not including rest stops.
Best Times: Daily 10am to sunset.
Worst Times: Early mornings and late evenings, when some of the sites visited on this walk are closed.

In 1779, James Boswell wrote to lexicographer Dr. Johnson ". . . here again I am in a state of much enjoyment . . . Chester pleases my fancy more than any town I ever saw." Two centuries later, Chester still delights. Within the town's medieval walls are black and white buildings from most every historical age, charming balcony-fronted streets, and seemingly endless uneven rows of double-tiered shops.

Today, Chester is Britain's only completely walled city. The town was first encircled with stone by the Romans, then extended by the Saxons. By the early Middle Ages, the city wall was dotted with numerous defensive towers and gateways. Following the 17th-century

English Civil War, the walls were altered to incorporate a popular wall-top promenade that can still be strolled today.

Chester has undergone heavy restoration and reconstruction, making it one of the most pleasant English cities to explore on foot.

Begin your walk at:

1. **The Cross,** at the intersection of Northgate, Eastgate, Watergate, and Bridge streets. The Cross has been the literal and figurative center of Chester's life ever since the 1st century A.D., when the Romans laid-out the city's rectangular street plan. The Cross itself was erected on this site in 1407, alongside a fountain that flowed with wine on saints days and other festive occasions. And it was here that the town crier read proclamations to passersby, daily at noon and 3pm. For centuries, The Cross marked the center of city government, and was the spot where merchants bargained and traded. Destroyed in the mid-17th century during the English Civil War, The Cross was restored in 1975; the same time in which the area you are now standing was closed to vehicular traffic.

   The building behind The Cross is:

2. **The Church of St. Peter,** one of Chester's oldest, founded in A.D. 907. Enter the church and examine the pillar that's closest to you. The niche in the column once contained a statue of the Virgin Mary, destroyed during the 17th-century English Civil War by Oliver Cromwell's Parliamentarian soldiers. The column itself is decorated with the remains of a religious painting of unknown antiquity. The artwork was plastered over by Cromwell's soldiers in the belief that they were destroying it. In reality, however, the plaster helped to preserve the art, and the mural has now been restored to something approaching its original state.

   Exit the church, turn right, and walk straight ahead onto Watergate Street, a road that contains many of the crypts, or cellars, that are typical of Chester. The third building on your left is:

3. **God's Providence House,** named for the inscription painted on its facade that reads "Gods Providence is Mine Inheritance." The house dates from 1652. The inscription is believed to have been written by the home's original owner, a man who escaped infection during the outbreak of bubonic plague that swept Chester in the 17th century. Plans to demolish the house in 1862 provoked public outcry, and the house instead was restored to its

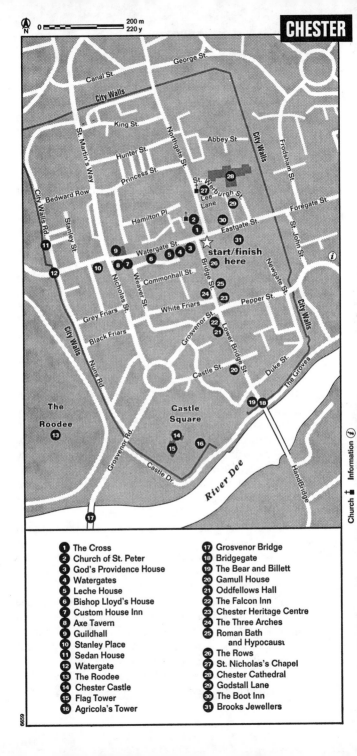

CHESTER

0   200 m
    220 y

George St.

Canal St.

City Walls

King St.

St. Martin's Way

Hunter St.

Abbey St.

City Walls

Frodsham St.

Princess St.

St. Werburgh St.

Bedward Row

② ㉗

㉖

Lee Lane

㉙

Foregate St.

City Walls Rd.

Hamilton Pl.

② ㉚

St. John St.

Stanley St.

①

Eastgate St.

⑪

⑨

Watergate St.

③

㉛

Information ⓘ

⑧⑦

⑥ ⑤④

★ start/finish here

⑫

⑩

Nicholas St.

Weaver St.

Commonhall St.

㉖

Bridge St.

Newgate St.

Grey Friars

White Friars

㉕

㉔

㉓

Pepper St.

City Walls

Black Friars

City Walls

Nuns Rd.

Grosvenor St.

㉒

㉑

Lower Bridge St.

Castle St.

⑳

Duke St.

The Groves

The Roodee

⑬

Castle Square

⑲⑱

Grosvenor Rd.

⑭

⑮ ⑯

Castle Dr.

River Dee

HandBridge

⑰

Church ✝   Information ⓘ

① The Cross
② Church of St. Peter
③ God's Providence House
④ Watergates
⑤ Leche House
⑥ Bishop Lloyd's House
⑦ Custom House Inn
⑧ Axe Tavern
⑨ Guildhall
⑩ Stanley Place
⑪ Sedan House
⑫ Watergate
⑬ The Roodee
⑭ Chester Castle
⑮ Flag Tower
⑯ Agricola's Tower

⑰ Grosvenor Bridge
⑱ Bridgegate
⑲ The Bear and Billett
⑳ Gamull House
㉑ Oddfellows Hall
㉒ The Falcon Inn
㉓ Chester Heritage Centre
㉔ The Three Arches
㉕ Roman Bath and Hypocaust
㉖ The Rows
㉗ St. Nicholas's Chapel
㉘ Chester Cathedral
㉙ Godstall Lane
㉚ The Boot Inn
㉛ Brooks Jewellers

6659

original state. The revitalization included enlarging the home's windows and adding pargetting—decorative plasterwork that no longer exists on any other building in Chester.

The building next door to God's Providence House is:

4. **Watergates,** an impressive crypt, considered the finest in Chester, and now a very atmospheric pub. Standing on the former site of Roman-era buildings, it was once the cellar of a prestigious medieval town house that was built for an extremely wealthy merchant. You can enter the crypt and see evidence of medieval timber partitioning that once separated the basement into several distinct rooms. It is likely that each room operated as an individual shop. Shop and work space was in short supply on what was once Chester's busiest commercial street—the main thoroughfare connecting the nearby river docks with the town center. Over the years, shopkeepers occupying these quarters have included fishmongers, potters, tanners, apothecaries, and vintners.

Exit Watergates, continue walking along Watergate Street, and turn left up the stairs, to:

5. **The Leche House,** one of Chester's oldest surviving houses and one of England's best-preserved examples of 15th-century architecture. The house is named for John Leche, the home's 17th-century owner.

At the time of this writing, Leche House stands empty. A peek through one of the building's ground-floor windows provides visitors with a good idea of what an Elizabethan domestic interior looked like. The home's primary ground-floor room is two stories high, and contains an ornate fireplace decorated with the extremely colorful Leche family coat of arms. The curious-looking cavity to the right of the fireplace may have been a "Priests' Hole," a place where persecuted Catholic priests could have hidden during Elizabethan times.

Continue walking along Watergate Street. On your left will be:

6. **Bishop Lloyd's House,** 41 Watergate Street, a home built in 1615 for the bishop of Chester. The house is Chester's finest example of centuries-old carved timberwork. The best way to view the home's magnificent exterior is to cross to the other side of Watergate Street. From here you can clearly see the carved panels which depict biblical subjects. Updated to 17th-century tastes, the carvings portray Abraham, dressed as a Jacobean gentleman, about to sacrifice his son Isaac.

Walk one block further along Watergate Street. On your left, at the junction of Weaver Street, is:

7. Custom House Inn, a 1637 town house built for Thomas and
Anne Weaver—you can see the couple's initials carved on the
building facade. Now a pub, Custom House Inn was enlarged in
the 18th century, incorporating the house next door.

One block further along Watergate Street, at the junction of
Nicholas Street, is:

8. The Axe Tavern, a public house once known as the Yacht Inn
where Dean Jonathan Swift, author of *Gulliver's Travels,* once
lodged. While staying here, Swift invited several dignitaries from
the nearby cathedral to dine with him. The clerics refused and
the offended Swift used his diamond ring to etch the following
lines on one of the inn's windows:

> *Rotten without and mouldering within,*
> *This place and its clergy are both near akin.*

The building opposite the Axe Tavern is:

9. Guildhall, the headquarters of the city's guilds which regulated
trade and tradesmen. Apprenticeship to a member of a guild was
the only way in medieval times to learn the skills necessary for
the practice of a trade or craft; each guild rigorously protected its
particular trade secret or "mystery." The guilds organized
regular performances of so-called Mystery Plays, cycles drama-
tizing the Bible from the creation to the last judgment, that were
once an important part of English life. Fully developed early in
the 14th century, the plays probably began as a means of making
the Latin-language teachings of the church accessible to an
illiterate general public. They were meant to entertain as well as
educate. Plays from these cycles are still occasionally staged,
usually at The Cross (see Stop 1, above).

The Guildhall you are standing in front of is located in a
converted, 19th-century deconsecrated church.

Cross Nicholas Street—a road that was once known as "Pill
Box Promenade" because so many of its houses were occupied
by doctors—and continue along Watergate Street to:

10. Stanley Place, a black-and-white timber-framed building that
was once home to one of Chester's richest families. Built in
1591, and augmented around 1700, the building's owners held
the right to collect taxes on all goods that passed through
Chester's Watergate—the city gate closest to the River Dee.
Stanley Place has been restored to its 18th-century splendor, and
is open to the public Monday through Wednesday, Friday, and
Saturday from 10am to noon and again from 2 to 5pm. It's

closed Thursdays and Sundays. There is a small admission charge.

Walk one more block along Watergate Street then turn right onto Stanley Street. Two blocks ahead, turn left onto Stanley Place and walk to the street's end to:

11. Sedan House, a home named for its large cubicle doorway. Known as a "Sedan Porch," the house's entrance was designed to accommodate a sedan chair—a means of transportation that could be hired in the 18th century, a chair carried on vertical poles by two bearers. This home's unusual design allowed the chair's wealthy passenger to enter the house directly from the sedan, without getting cold or wet.

Turn left onto City Walls Road and walk one block to:

12. Watergate, the portal in Chester's city wall through which traders accessed the Port of Chester. Active since the Middle Ages, when trading ships brought cloth from Germany, armor from Italy, and wine from France and Spain, the gate has long been an important part of Chester city life. The current gate dates from 1788.

Climb up the stairs onto the City Wall Walkway and look across to:

13. The Roodee, Chester's racehorse track. The racetrack's name comes from the Saxon words "rood eye," meaning "island of the cross." Remains of an artificial, Roman-era stone harbor that were found here prove that the River Dee once flowed past the racecourse, directly beneath the city walls. Races were held on these meadows as early as 1540, making Roodee England's oldest race course. Scornfully criticized by 19th-century critics as a "soup plate," Roodee is certainly one of the most unusual race courses in the world. The track's 1 mile, 49 yard layout—practically all on a curve—makes it possible for spectators to easily view the entire race without the help of binoculars. And although this is an advantage to spectators, many horses have difficulty getting used to the tightness of the course, a cramped loop that gives inside horses a distinct advantage.

Walk along the City Wall Walkway all the way to its end, then descend the steps and turn left onto busy Grosvenor Road. After one long block, turn right into Castle Square. Just past the statue of a somewhat homely looking Queen Victoria, turn right, through the archway, into:

14. Chester Castle, located in the southernmost corner of the walled city. The castle was begun by William the Conqueror who, after crowning himself king in 1066, wasted no time marching north to rout the indigenous insurgents. Chester fell in

1069, and this castle was immediately begun, probably on the site of a former Saxon fortress. The hereditary earldom of Chester was created first for Gherbod, a Fleming, and then for William's nephew, Hugh d'Avranches, who was known as "The Wolf" because of his ruthless character and his barbarous conquest of North Wales.

Turn left, through the doorway to the former castle guard-room, a building constructed in 1846 that now houses an exhibition detailing the history of Chester Castle. The three jail cells in the guardroom were constructed to house unruly soldiers. Each has a stout wooden door with a peephole and hatch, through which food and drink could be passed to the prisoners. A metal flag fixed to the corridor wall, could be raised from inside the cells for the purpose of attracting the attention of the prisoner's guards.

Exit the guardroom, turn left, and walk across the cobble-stones and up the ramp to:

15. Flag Tower, a 12th-century stone defensive tower built to replace a wooden fortress that once stood here. Constructed of massive, seven-foot-thick walls the tower has been altered over the years, losing its original battlements and roof.

Just ahead, a rather atmospheric staircase, reeking of stale urine, provides visitors with a startling impression of what the castle's less hygienic past may have been like.

Exit the tower and walk around the castle's battlements to:

16. Agricola's Tower, a 12th-century structure comprising three square towers originally intended to operate as the castle gatehouse. Enter the tower via the vaulted entranceway that at one time contained wooden gates and a guarded bridge. The gates were bricked up in the 13th century. In the 17th century, Agricola's Tower was utilized as a storage facility for ammuni-tion and gunpowder, a function it continued to serve until 1909.

Make your way up the very uneven staircase and peer through the doorway at the Chapel of St. Mary de Castro, a small church dating from the late 12th or early 13th century. Reinforced in 1301 by Edward, Earl of Chester, for the purpose of protecting his treasure, the chapel's altar is now recessed into the thick wall. The church's outstanding wall paintings—reminiscent of manuscript illuminations in their small scale—were only recently discovered, during a 1992 restoration. The paintings, dating from the first half of the 13th century, are the most significant medieval wall paintings in northwest England.

Exit Agricola's Tower, then exit Chester Castle through the arch where you entered. Turn left onto Grosvenor Road, then left again onto Castle Drive. After about a block, climb the stairs on your left onto the City Wall Walkway and look right, at:

17. Grosvenor Bridge. When this magnificent segmental arch was completed in 1833, it was the largest single stone arch in the world. Critics of the project confidently predicted that the bridge would soon collapse.

Continue walking along the City Wall Walkway as it turns to the left. When the wall takes a sharp right turn, descend the steps, and bear left onto Castle Drive, the road that runs alongside the River Dee. After a long block, turn left onto Lower Bridge Street, pausing at:

18. Bridgegate, the city wall's southeasternmost portal. This medieval entrance was originally flanked by two defensive towers. The water tower that now stands here was built in 1601 to supply piped water to the city. The present archway was built in 1782.

Continue along Lower Bridge Street and pause outside the second building on your left. This is:

19. The Bear and Billett, an 18th-century pub that was once the town house of the earl of Shrewsbury. This outstanding wooden building dates from 1664 and may have replaced an earlier structure destroyed during the English Civil War. Look up at the second story, where a door is set into the house's gable. The door provides easy access into the house's attic, and was once used to deliver storage items. The pub's windows contain over 1,000 panes of glass.

Two blocks ahead on Lower Bridge Street, walk up the stairs on your left onto Gamull Terrace and pause outside Benson's Bistro and Restaurant. The eatery is inside:

20. Gamull House, a Jacobean building that was once the home of Sir Francis Gamull, the mayor of Chester from 1635 to 1636. A supporter of the Royalists during the English Civil War, Gamull entertained King Charles I here in 1645, from September 23rd to the 25th, during the battle of Rowton Moor.

Return to Lower Bridge Street and walk one more block to:

REFUELING STOP   Ye Old King's Head, Lower Bridge Street (tel. 0244/324855). Built sometime around 1633, this rustic pub was once the home of Randle Holme, the first mayor of Chester, who served from 1633 to 1634. Four generations of the Holme family worked as messengers and historians during the 17th century.

The pub serves food Monday through Saturday from 11am to 2pm, as well as several different kinds of "real" live ales.

Continue along Lower Bridge Street, noting the Tudor house on your right which dates from 1503. One block ahead, on your left, is:

21. Oddfellows Hall, a meeting hall constructed in the early 18th century as a mansion for John Williams, the attorney general of Cheshire.

Continue to the end of Lower Bridge Street, where it intersects Grosvenor Street, to:

22. The Falcon Inn, a pub that was originally built in the 17th century as a town house for Thomas Grosvenor, Duke of Westminster. When Grosvenor married Mary Davies, heiress to London's Ebury Estate (encompassing modern Belgravia and Mayfair), the foundations were laid for what is perhaps the greatest fortune in England. Indeed, the present duke is believed to be the wealthiest man in England.

Cross Pepper Street onto Bridge Street. The building on the far right corner of this intersection is:

23. The Chester Heritage Centre, a historical museum located inside the deconsecrated St. Michael's Church. The church, one of nine medieval parish churches in Chester, stands on the former site of the southernmost gateway of the original Roman fortress. Almost completely rebuilt from 1849 to 1851, the oldest remaining part of St. Michael's is the beautifully carved chancel roof, which dates from 1496.

The building was transformed into the present day Heritage Center in 1975. Inside are displays on city history and architecture, as well as a 20-minute audiovisual presentation featuring over 300 slides chronicling Chester's past.

The Chester Heritage Centre is open Monday through Saturday from 11am to 5pm and Sunday from noon to 5pm. There is a small admission charge.

Exit the Heritage Centre and turn right onto Bridge Street. Almost immediately on your left, you'll see:

24. The Three Arches, 13th-century ruins that once formed the facade of a row medieval building. These arches are believed to be the oldest surviving shop fronts in England. The structure behind the arches, once an impressive stone town house, dates from the early to mid-14th century.

Walk one more block along Bridge Street, walk through the Spud-U-Like shop on your right, then turn left and descend the steps to:

25. The Roman Bath and Hypocaust, 1st-century relics that lie in an almost perfect state of preservation. More than 1,800 years old, the bath was an important meeting and washing place that was constructed in most every Roman city. The Hypocaust was a group of evenly spaced squat, square stone columns that measured about two feet high. A floor was laid atop the columns and hot air was blown up through the floor from a furnace positioned underneath—perhaps an example of the first known type of central heating.

Return to Bridge Street and turn right. Notice the shops and houses on your right that are elevated several feet above street level. These are known collectively as:

26. The Rows. You have probably noticed this unusual architecture throughout your walk. The Rows are unique to Chester and are one of the city's most famous features. Some historians believe that The Rows were the result of deliberate city planning in the 13th century. It seems more likely, however, that The Rows were created gradually between the 13th and 18th centuries.

A two-block walk along Bridge Street Row will return you to The Cross. Turn right at The Cross, then left onto Northgate Street. After one long block, turn right, into the small covered passageway called Lee Lane. At the end of the passageway, look to your left at the remains of:

27. St. Nicholas's Chapel, a medieval church that was transformed in 1777 into the Theatre Royal, and later, into the Chester Music Hall. A stop on Charles Dickens's national reading tour, the music hall hosted the writer in 1867. Dickens was seriously ill when he arrived in Chester. He told his doctor that he felt "giddy, with a tendency to go backwards, and to turn round. . . ." He also spoke of some strangeness of his left hand and arm. A close friend would recall that Dickens's "mind was more disturbed by it than his manner would lead anyone . . . to suppose," Medical historians believe that Dickens had suffered a mild paralytic stroke, but the author carried on with his reading tour all the same.

With your back to St. Nicholas's Chapel, cross St. Werburgh Street to:

28. Chester Cathedral, the town's largest church and religious seat. The cathedral's story begins with Werburgh, the daughter of the Mercian king, born in A.D. 650. Werburgh became first a nun, then an abbess, and was widely known for her piety. After Werburgh's death, miracles at her tomb were soon reported.

When the residents of Chester were forced to build a fortress here against invading Norsemen in 907, they brought Werburgh's remains to the town in the belief that the bones would help protect them. A church dedicated to St. Werburgh was built on the site of the present cathedral, which was later, in 1092, to become part of a Benedictine monastery.

Enter the cathedral and walk straight through the church to the cloistered courtyard. The fountain in the center of this small garden was once a reservoir; the recesses between the columns around the courtyard's perimeter were used as carrels—or private study areas—where the monks worked copying manuscripts.

Walk around the cloisters, turn right at the bookshop, and walk straight toward the doorway that's in front of you. The room on your left is the parlour, which now functions as the practice room for the cathedral choir.

Turn left, into the refectory, a 13th-century dining hall that accommodated about 40 monks thrice daily. During meals, one monk would read from the magnificent stone pulpit. The fine 17th-century tapestry on the west wall depicts a scene from the Acts of the Apostles, based on a cartoon by Raphael.

Retrace your footsteps to the cloisters, turn right and enter the abbot's burial place, where Benedictine leaders were entombed as early as 1092.

Farther around the cloisters, turn left through the door and walk back into the cathedral. Once inside, turn left again, and walk to the monument of John Pearson, bishop of Chester from 1672 to 1686. A great theologian, Pearson played a prominent role in the dialogues that led to the adoption of the official prayer book of the Church of England.

Turn left, into the north transept, the round arch of which is the oldest part of this cathedral, dating from 1100. The small doorway to the left of the arch connected the monks' dormitory to the cathedral.

Make your way to the choir—the "top" end of the church. Dating from the end of the 13th century, the choir contains some magnificently carved stalls, over which is a tabernacle (or canopy) to shelter worshipers from cold drafts that whistled down from the unglazed windows above. Each canopy is slightly different, and supported by tiny carved corbels. The carvings depict a variety of subjects including the birth of Christ, biblical subjects, animals and birds, and human acrobats. Each of the seats in the stalls can be turned up, revealing ledges called misericords, from the Latin word *misericordia,* meaning "pity," and intended to support those unable to stand for long periods during services. The carvings on the misericords are both imaginative and humorous, and include men wrestling, couples arguing, foxes stealing grapes, and a wide variety of monsters.

Exit the Chester Cathedral, cross St. Werburgh Street, and walk straight, onto:

29. **Godstall Lane,** one of only four medieval lanes to survive intact within the city's walls. Long an important route leading to the Abbey of St. Werburgh, Godstall means "God's place."

At the end of Godstall Lane, turn right, onto Dark Row, the elevated row above Eastgate Street, still looking very much the way it did in the 18th century, when the then run-down row was known to be a dangerous place after sundown. A few doors down you'll see:

30. **The Boot Inn,** a 17th-century pub that was once Chester's best-known brothel. Enter The Boot, which was restored in the 1980s. Just past the door, notice an exposed section of the inn's original wattle-and-daub construction.

Exit The Boot Inn, descend the steps onto Eastgate Street, and walk straight across the street to:

REFUELING STOP   The Crypt, Eastgate Street (tel. 024/435-0001, ext. 273). A subterranean pub dating from the 13th century, The Crypt's atmospheric setting is a good place to enjoy a light snack and a cold pint. Specializing in salads and ploughman's lunches—bread, cheese, and chutney plates— The Crypt serves meals daily from 11am to 4pm.

Exit The Crypt, turn right onto Eastgate Street, climb the steps on your right, and turn right to:

31. **Brooks Jewellers,** a gem and bangle shop. The shop dates from the 17th century; these premises have been occupied by jewellers for over 400 years and the coats of arms of craftsmen past are depicted in the stained glass of the shop's windows. Enter the store and ask a member of the staff to escort you to their magnificent Oak Room. The room's carved mantelpiece dates from 1664 and depicts the rustic Port of Chester.

Back on Eastgate Street, turn left. Walk one long block and you will return to The Cross, where you began this tour.

WALKING TOUR 9

York Part I

Start: York British Rail Station, Station Road.
Finish: York Minster, Minster Yard.
Time: 2½ hours, not including rest stops.
Best Times: Daily 10am to 4:30pm, when the buildings on this tour are open.
Worst Times: Early mornings and late evenings, when many of the sights are closed.

York is a wonderful city to explore—its history is literally written in the streets. This first walk will take you to York Minster, one of the great cathedrals of the world, and the largest in England, memorable for its stained glass which has survived the vicissitudes of the Reformation, the English Civil War, and several fires and other disasters.

Our two walks will take you via backstreets and passageways, through the pageant of English history. Some of these streets are too small to appear on the map; they are known as the "snickelways"— curious twisty, tiny passages that pass behind and beside the major thoroughfares, and lead to hidden city streets. They can easily be found by following the directions given in the walks.

As King George VI famously observed, "The history of York is the history of England."

Begin your tour at York British Rail Station. Turn left out of the station and walk toward the River Ouse on Station Road. After about two blocks, bear right just before the white statue, walk through the arch, and turn left up the stairs onto the City Wall. Walk atop the City Wall all the way to the river. Cross Lendal Bridge into Museum Street. After about two blocks, turn left onto the unnamed street located just past the telephone boxes. Walk through the gates to the ruins of:

1. **St. Leonard's Hospital,** a medieval infirmary that was once the largest hospital in northern England. Founded in the 10th century and named St. Peter's Hospital, the building was re-founded as St. Leonard's by King Stephen (1097–1154). St. Leonard's flourished as an important medical institution until it was closed by King Henry VIII during his dissolution of the monasteries, in 1540.

   All that remains of the building today is an ancient chapel above a vaulted crypt. Continue along the pathway which ends at the:

2. **Multangular Tower,** a 4th-century defensive tower that once formed the northwest corner of *Eboracum,* a Roman-era fortress that once stood here.

   Turn right onto another path, passing, on your right, the remains of the boundary wall of St. Leonard's Hospital. Turn left up the four steps, then left again along the stony path. Turn right through the gate, follow the gravel path to the end, then turn right again to the ruins of:

3. **St. Mary's Abbey.** Once one of the largest abbeys in England, Benedictine St. Mary's was built in 1089, and reconstructed in the 14th century. The ruins you see here date from this later period, but are still over 600 years old. In its day, St. Mary's was one of the region's wealthiest and most powerful foundations. The abbey was dissolved by King Henry VIII in 1539, along with other holdings.

   Follow the path through the ruins, and stay with it as it goes down a hill and to the right. Walk through the gates, turn right onto Marygate, and walk straight for about four blocks, passing 11th-century St. Olave's Church on your right. Along the way, notice the:

4. **Wooden Parapet Shutters** on the defensive wall to your right. These shutters are actually reproductions of the type of

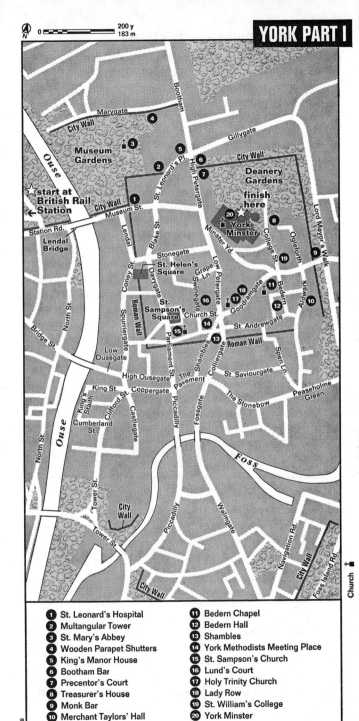

0 — 200 y / 183 m

N

Ouse

Marygate
City Wall

Museum
Gardens

start at British Rail Station

Station Rd.
Lendal Bridge

City Wall
Museum St.

Bootham

Gillygate

City Wall

Deanery Gardens

finish here

York Minster

Lord Mayor's Walk

Ogleforth

College St.

Bedern

Aldwark

St. Leonard's Pl.
High Petergate

Minster Yd.

Low Petergate

Stonegate

Grape Ln.

St. Helen's Square

Swinegate

St. Sampson's Square

Church St.

Goodramgate

St. Andrewgate

Roman Wall

Parliament St.

The Shambles

Pavement

Coppergate

Piccadilly

Fossgate

Collergate

St. Saviourgate

The Stonebow

Peaseholme Green

Spen Ln.

Foss

Ouse

North St.

Bridge St.

Low Ousegate

High Ousegate

King St.
King's Staith
Clifford St.
Cumberland St.
Castlegate

Tower St.

City Wall

City Wall

Walmgate

Navigation Rd.

City Wall

Fos's Island Rd.

Church

Blake St.
Coney St.
Davygate
Spurriergate
Roman Wall

Lendal

Marygate

Precentor's Court

Legend:

1. St. Leonard's Hospital
2. Multangular Tower
3. St. Mary's Abbey
4. Wooden Parapet Shutters
5. King's Manor House
6. Bootham Bar
7. Precentor's Court
8. Treasurer's House
9. Monk Bar
10. Merchant Taylors' Hall
11. Bedern Chapel
12. Bedern Hall
13. Shambles
14. York Methodists Meeting Place
15. St. Sampson's Church
16. Lund's Court
17. Holy Trinity Church
18. Lady Row
19. St. William's College
20. York Minster

6660

shutters that existed here during medieval times. Their purpose was to safeguard the city's longbowman against being struck by enemy arrows. Immediately after a bowman fired his arrows— each in quick succession—the wooden shutter would be swung down to protect him. Although the shutters you see here are modern, they sit in the wall's original 13th- and 14th-century grooves. These grooves do not exist anywhere else in York, and it is doubtful that there are many others like them anywhere in England.

At the end of Marygate turn right, onto Bootham, a street named from an old Scandinavian word *buthum,* meaning an area of temporary dwellings. At the second set of traffic lights, turn right onto St. Leonard's Place and walk to the:

5. **King's Manor House,** constructed in 1280 as a residence for the abbot of St. Mary's Abbey, and enlarged in 1490. Henry VIII stayed here with Anne Boleyn, and later with Catherine Howard. Charles I was here in 1633 and 1639, and Charles II was also here.

Walk through the Manor House's gates to the main entrance. Notice the coat of arms of King Charles I above the doorway. The unicorn represents Scotland, the lion symbolizes England, and the harp Ireland. The flags on the lances, held by a pair of beasts, are the standards of St. Andrew and St. George. On the royal coat of arms, the French fleur-de-lys reminds us that until the reign of George III, kings of England claimed to be also kings of France.

Go into the courtyard and walk along the pathway, where on the left is:

REFUELING STOP The King's Manor Refectory, King's Manor House. The original manor dining room is still in use, open to the public as a small restaurant. The Refectory serves coffee and light snacks from 10am to noon, English-style lunches from noon to 2pm, and afternoon tea from 2 to 4pm.

Exit King's Manor House and cross Exhibition Square, turn right at the traffic lights and cross over the road. On your left is:

6. **Bootham Bar,** a gate across High Petergate that once controlled access to York from points northwest. In York, all gates are called "bars," a term that may have derived from the word "barrier." The oldest of York's gates is Bootham Bar, dating from the 11th century. In medieval times, guards posted on the

bar defended visitors arriving from the nearby Forest of Galtres from roving packs of wolves.

Walk through the left arch of the bar onto High Petergate and, just before the Hole in the Wall pub, turn left onto the unmarked alley to:

7. Precentor's Court, a bucolic street dating from 1610. One of the nicest lanes in York, Precentor's Court has remained an exceptional haven of quietude for over 350 years. The street is lined with elegant buildings and old gas lamps outside each of them. A precentor was a church officer in charge of the choir, an important position. Precentors often took their jobs very seriously; one medieval York precentor sent his choirboys to prison for singing rude words to the anthem

Turn right onto Precentor's Court, then turn left through the gates into Deanery Gardens. Take the pathway that forks right, walk across the park, then turn right onto Minster Yard. After about one block, turn left onto Chapter House Street and walk to the:

8. Treasurer's House (tel. 0904/624247), the former home of the treasurer of York Minster. The first treasurer's house to stand on this site was built around the year 1100 for an occupant named Radulphus. Treasurers, who were appointed by the church, were employed until the dissolution of the monasteries, when York Minster, along with England's other churches, was stripped of its treasures by King Henry VIII. York Minster's last treasurer, William Clyffe, retained his title for seven more years, but in 1546, Clyffe decided that he had had enough. He resigned with his famous philosophical words *abrepto omni thesauro, desuit thesaurarii munus,* meaning "there being no treasure left, there would seem to be no need for a treasurer."

When Clyffe left, this building became a private house, and was largely rebuilt between 1628 and 1648. It was from a window in this house in the 18th century that the 21-year-old deaf-and-dumb astronomer, John Goodrich, invented a technique of measuring distances of objects in the universe. The elegant rooms of the Treasurer's House now shelter a delightful collection of antique furnishings and fittings. There is a small admission charge.

Exit Treasurer's House and continue walking along Chapter House Street. After one block, the street bends right and changes its name to Ogleforth. Turn left onto Goodramgate and walk one block to:

9. Monks Bar, the tallest of York's city gates. Named for the monks of a nearby monastery, and designed in such a way that it was possible to defend each floor even if the others had been taken, 63-foot-high Monks Bar was the city's strongest defensive gate.

Walk through the gate and look back at it. The statues of giants on the very top are as fearsome as the gate itself. The hulking figure on the left holds a boulder, and seems as though it is ready to throw it down upon the heads of foolish invaders.

Backtrack along the left side of Goodramgate, turning left onto the first street, Aldwark. Three blocks ahead, on your left, is the:

10. **Merchant Taylors' Hall,** the headquarters of the association of tailors, drapers, and hosiers. In 1662, King Charles II granted a royal charter which allowed for the incorporation of the three medieval guilds. The guilds, which were closely tied to the church, were responsible for the licensing and regulation of craftsmen. The building that the Merchant Taylors occupied dates from 1386, and is open to the public from May through September, Monday through Friday from 10am to 4pm. Admission is free.

Exit Merchant Taylors' Hall, backtrack to Goodramgate, and turn left. Take the first left into a very small passage called Bedern, and pause at the first building on your right. This is the remains of:

11. **Bedern Chapel,** the church of the College of the Vicar's Choral, consecrated in 1349. The name "Bedern" is Anglo-Saxon in origin, and means "house of prayer." By the mid-19th century, the region around the chapel had deteriorated into a dreadful slum, rampant with poverty and disease. As you can see, the area has changed significantly, and now contains tasteful modern dwellings.

Continue along Bedern and turn right onto Bartle Garth. Half a block ahead, on your left, is:

12. **Bedern Hall,** the former refectory of the vicar's choral, founded in the 14th century. The hall is only open to the public on the first Monday of each month; March through September from 10am to 6pm, and October through February from 10am to 4pm.

Walk to the end of Bartle Garth, turn right onto St. Andrewgate, and continue about two blocks to King's Square. Walk to the far left corner of the square, pausing at the street called:

13. **Shambles.** This ancient street of butchers is the only York thoroughfare to be mentioned in the Domesday Book, William the Conqueror's 11th-century survey of his real-estate holdings.

The street takes its name from the word *Shamel,* a Saxon term relating to the stalls or benches on which meat was displayed. Contemporary versions of the Shamel can still be seen here. The road was laid out around the year 1400; houses were built on either side in order to block the meat-spoiling sun. Overcrowding, bad water, and poor sanitation rendered the Shambles an ideal breeding ground for the plague and pestilence that frequently devastated York between the 12th and 17th centuries.

With Shambles on your left, walk straight onto Newgate Street. The building on your right, at the junction of Patrickpool Lane, was the:

14. **York Methodists Meeting Place** from 1753 to 1759. Gathering in the building's upper story, the Methodists were sometimes led in prayer by the religion's founders John and Charles Wesley.

Turn right onto Patrickpool Lane and walk past:

15. **St. Sampson's Church,** a relatively unspectacular chapel that dates from 1154. The building's tower was damaged by cannonballs in 1644, and the church was almost completely rebuilt in 1848.

Walk across St. Sampson's Square—a former produce market that was known as "Thursday Market"—onto Three Cranes Lane. Turn left onto Swinegate, and after a short block, turn right onto the very narrow lane called:

16. **Lund's Court.** The passageway was formerly known as "Mad Alice Lane," named for a woman who lived here named Alice Smith who was deemed insane and hanged for it at York Castle in 1825.

Walk to the end of Lund's Court, a very low passageway that may prove difficult to those over 5 feet 6 inches tall. Walk almost directly across the street called Low Petergate into another alleyway called Hornpot Lane, a 13th-century passageway named for hornmakers who used to work in this area. Hornpot Lane ends at:

17. **Holy Trinity Church,** a delightful, hidden 13th-century church that is missed by most visitors to York. Enter the church, turn right along the first aisle, then right again into the side chapel. Added to the church sometime during the 15th century, the chapel was funded with a bequest by Robert de Howne. Here the de Howne family could attend private masses conducted by a specially hired priest. These masses were held at the same time that the general mass was going on in the church's main body. In order that the private service could be timed with that of the high altar, the chapel was fitted with a hagioscope, a

peep hole in the wall to the left of the chapel's altar. If you peer through it, you can look straight at the church's high altar.

Exit the chapel and make your way to the church's main altar, above which is a stained-glass window dating from 1471. A gift to the church from its rector, John Walker, this window is one of the rare survivals of both the Protestant Reformation and the English Civil War. John Walker is shown kneeling in the center; on the right is the Holy Trinity, and the Holy Spirit, depicted as a dove, hovers above the Father, who is holding the Corpus Christi.

Walk down the church's central aisle to the interesting double-tierd pulpit on your left. Purchased for £6 in 1695, the pulpit is surrounded by several uneven pews, each of which open up for storage. You can look inside them. These irregular pews were bought and installed by individual parishioners in the 17th and 18th centuries.

Exit Holy Trinity Church, continuing along the pathway to Goodramgate. Turn left onto Goodramgate. This section of the street is known as:

18. Lady Row, and is the oldest surviving row of houses in York. Built in 1316, the structures are also the earliest English examples of architecture where the upper floor project beyond the lower. The houses on Lady Row were constructed for the purpose of raising funds to pay for a priest for the nearby church of St. Mary. After King Henry VIII's dissolution of the monasteries in 1539 to 1540, the row became the property of the City of York, which now rents these houses as shops.

Walk two blocks along Goodramgate to:

REFUELING STOP Four Seasons, 45 Goodramgate (tel. 0904/633787). A beamed, medieval hall dating from the 16th century, Four Seasons specializes in homemade specialties such as traditional English pasties, roasts, and steak-and-mushroom pie. Mercifully, no smoking is permitted.

Continue to the end of Goodramgate and walk under the wooden-framed building into College Street. One block ahead, on your right, is:

19. St. William's College, a religious school built in 1465 to house young priests. Finding themselves with a lot of time on their hands between the twice daily masses, the well-paid 15th-century junior priests acquired a reputation around town for being quite troublesome; violent clashes between the priests and the townsfolk became common. In the hope that keeping the young priests off the streets would also keep them out of trouble, the dean of York Minster decided to provide his charges with a place to live and study. To this end, St. William's was established. The college is dedicated to William Fitzherbert, the great-grandson of William the Conqueror, who was archbishop of York in 1153.

The college is only occasionally open to the public; when it is open, it's worth a look around.

With your back to St. William's College, walk towards York Minster along the flagstone path. Turn right into Minster Yard and follow it around to the main entrance of:

20. York Minster one of England's greatest cathedrals. Constructed atop the ruins of a former Norman cathedral, the present building was begun by Archbishop Walter de Gray in 1220, took 250 years to complete, and is England's largest cathedral.

Enter the cathedral, walk up the central aisle and look back at the Great West Window, a stained-glass masterpiece dating from 1338. Commissioned by Archbishop Melton, the predominately red-and-gold glass was created in a heart shape to represent the sacred heart of Christ. York Minster is unusual among English cathedrals in having retained much of its medieval stained glass. After the Protestant Reformation, the window's design was "reinterpreted," and it is still popularly known as "The Heart of Yorkshire."

Now face the altar, where high up on your left is a sculpture of a dragon that looks as if it's twisting awkwardly towards the ceiling. The dragon was probably positioned here as a kind of crane, used to lift a heavy cover off the font in the nave below. According to local legend, each night on the stroke of midnight, the dragon bows three times to the statue of St. George located across from it.

Walk to the far aisle, turn right, and take note of the Pilgrim's Window. The 14th-century stained glass depicts a knight and his lady setting off on a pilgrimage. Look closely at the window's borders, where secular and fanciful themes are explored. A scene at the bottom left shows monkeys conducting a funeral. The bottom center portrays a woman with a distaff (a piece of wood that holds the wool during spinning) chasing a fox with a goose, while on the bottom right is a hound being chased by a stag.

The adjacent window along is known as the Bellfounders' Window. Created in the early 1300s, the window was a gift to the Minster by Richard Tunnoc, a local bellfounder and dignitary. The stained glass commemorates the craft and skill of bell making; in the window's center is Tunnoc himself, presenting the window to the archbishop.

Turn left into the north transept and look up at the Five Sisters Window. This 13th-century stained-glass window with pointed arches is the best preserved example of early English grisaille, a gray-green glass decorated in a leaf pattern with inserted geometric medallions. Popular legend holds that the Five Sisters Window gets its name from a similarly designed tapestry created by five unmarried sisters. In reality, however, the window's story and name were the 19th-century inventions of novelist Charles Dickens who wrote about the Minster in his book *Nicholas Nickleby.*

Backtrack toward the north transept and turn right, into the aisle. The second monument you reach is the tomb of Prince William of Hatfield, the third child of King Edward III and Queen Phillipa of Hainault who were married in York Minster. William was only 10 years old when he died in 1344, and was buried here because both the king and queen had a personal affection for the Minster.

Further along the aisle, on your left, beside a little door, is the small Shield of the Minster Police Force. In 1829, John Martin, a member of a fanatical sect called the "Raters," became convinced that God wanted him to destroy York Minster, the pride of the Anglican church and, in his mind, the work of the devil. Martin hid in the cathedral when it closed on Sunday, February 1, 1829, and, when all was quiet, gathered together all the hassocks and prayer books he could find and set fire to them. The resulting conflagration destroyed much of the woodwork at the east end of the cathedral. As a result of Martin's actions the Minster Police Force was founded. To this day, 11 policemen are employed for the sole purpose of guarding the Minster, day and night. York Minster is the only church other than the Vatican to have its own police force.

Just past the Shield of the Minster Police Force, look up at the window on your left. This is the St. William Window, a 1422 stained-glass work depicting scenes from the life of St. William. It was no coincidence that William FitzHerbert, 12th-century archbishop of York was also the nephew of England's King Stephen and of Henry of Blois, the bishop of Winchester. His appointment, an act of blatant nepotism, scandalized the country. St. Bernard of Clarivaux, the church's leading Cistercian friar, had his own candidate for the post in Henry Murdac,

Chapter-house

Five Sisters Window

North Transept

Central Tower

Choir

Presbytery

Lady Chapel

East End

South Transept

Nave

West End

abbot of the Cistercian abbey of Fountains. He fired off a particularly unsaintly letter to the pope, in which he called Henry of Blois "the Whore of Winchester." No admirer of the Cistercians, Pope Lucius III disregarded St. Bernard, and William was appointed archbishop of York on September 26, 1143. When Pope Lucius III died four years later, his successor, Pope

Eugenius III promptly dismissed William FitzHerbert, replacing him with Henry Murdac. This divine soap opera came to an ironic conclusion in 1153, the year that Pope Eugenius, St. Bernard, and Henry Murdac all died. The new pope promptly reinstated William FitzHerbert, who returned in triumph as the archbishop of York.

When William collapsed during mass seven months later, rumors circulated claiming that the Cistercians had poisoned the archbishop's communion wine. The Cistercian leader, Archdeacon Osbert, resigned in disgrace, miracles were soon reported at William's tomb, and William was canonized a saint.

St. William's miracles are depicted on the stained-glass window you see here, along with almost 100 other scenes from his life. One of those pictured occurred here on an early 13th-century morning. During a service, a large stone dislodged from a pillar and fell on the head of a sleepy cleric who, "miraculously," was not killed. In 1867, a stone bearing the inscription "the stone which fell on the head of Roger of Ripon" was discovered outside York Minster. The rock, probably part of the shrine of St. William, may have been tossed out during the Reformation. The stone is now on display in The Foundations (see below).

Continue to the end of the aisle, turn right, and look left at the Great East Window, constructed from 1405 to 1408 and containing most of its medieval glass. It depicts the beginning and the end of the world, from Genesis to Revelations. The window is the work of John Thornton, a craftsman who was paid 4 shillings a week plus a £5 annual bonus for his work—a huge sum of money in those days. Thornton was also guaranteed a £10 bonus if he finished the window within three years, which he did.

Turn right into the next aisle and descend the steps into the crypt, for which there is a small admission charge. In early days, a crypt was simply a safe storage place for the treasures of a church. Later it was used to hold other treasures—human bones. York Minster crypt contains late Norman-era pillars and vaulting, as well as the coffin of St. William, which is actually a reused Roman sarcophagus—an ancient example of recycling.

Return upstairs, walk through the iron screen, and turn left, into the south transept. Look up at the 16th-century Rose Window. After Henry Tudor defeated Richard III at the Battle of Bosworth in 1485, he united the houses of York and Lancaster by marrying Elizabeth of York. The respective emblems of their royal houses—the red rose of Lancaster and the white rose of York—were brought together here by Flemish glaziers who arranged the red roses of the house of Lancaster with the red-and-white roses of the house of Tudor.

The monument to the left of the window is the tomb of Walter de Gray, the archbishop of York from 1215 to 1255. A powerful and respected member of government, de Gray was instrumental in the construction of York Minster. When the archbishop died, this elaborate tomb was erected. To this day, the memorial is considered to be the finest monument in York Minster; some even think it to be the finest of its kind in England.

To the right of the Rose Window is the entrance to The Foundations, the cathedral's ancient underpinnings that were only exposed within the last 30 years. Although there is a small admission charge, a visit to The Foundations is a must. The space was hastily excavated between 1967 and 1972 after it became apparent that York Minster's central tower was about to collapse. Engineers raced against time to secure the cathedral's substructure, sinking huge concrete collars that now support the tower. These can be viewed along with ancient remains that were discovered during the dig.

Upon exiting The Foundations you'll see the entrance to the tower on your right. It's worth climbing for terrific views over York. If you have the strength, continue your tour of the city with "Walking Tour 10—York Part II," which begins right here, at York Minster.

WALKING TOUR 10

York Part II

Start: York Minster, Minster Yard.
Finish: York Minster, Minster Yard.
Time: 1½ to 2 hours, not including rest stops.
Best Times: Daily 10am to 4:30pm, when the buildings on this tour are open.
Worst Times: Early mornings and late evenings, when many of the sights are closed.

Traces of its history as a Roman, then a Viking, and then a Norman city can be seen on this second walk through York. The Vikings called the city *Jorvick,* a name that was bastardized through the centuries to become "York." The Danes left an indelible mark on York—their street plan and place names still remain today. The ending "gate" on York's street names comes from the Scandinavian word *gata,* meaning street.

The walk also takes you through York's history as an important and flourishing medieval commercial and trading center. In the Middle Ages, York was also a favorite royal city, England's "second city," London, of course, being the first.

Five refueling stops are noted on the walk. While you may not feel you need that many stops for refreshment, each one is worth looking at for its historical interest.

With your back to the entrance of York Minster, cross Minster Yard and enter the:

1. **Church of St. Michael-le-Belfrey,** the only pre-Reformation church in York to be built from start to finish without stopping. Begun in 1525 by York Minster's master mason John Forman, the church's interior is an excellent example of early Tudor–style ecclesiastical architecture. A substantial amount of the church's stained glass dates from the 16th century; unusual due to the fact that most church glass was destroyed during the religious upheaval that came to be known as the Reformation. The church's east window dates from as early as 1330.

    Would-be political assassin Guy Fawkes was baptized in this church on April 16, 1570. A member of the Gunpowder Plot, a conspiracy to blow up King James and his Parliament, Fawkes is one of England's best-known infamous figures. When Guy Fawkes was 9 years old, his mother married a Roman Catholic, who brought up the young boy according to strict religious beliefs. When he turned 21, idealistic Guy enlisted in the Spanish army in Flanders, where he soon became disillusioned and cynical. Returning to England, he joined with fellow Roman Catholics Robert Catesby, Thomas Winwith, Thomas Percy, and John Wright in their plot to blow up Parliament; they reasoned that the ensuing turmoil would enable their co-religionists to take over the country, thereby acquiring the religious freedom they had been denied.

    The conspirators rented a cellar under London's Palace of Westminster where they hid several barrels of gunpowder. When an unknown person warned Lord Monteagle, brother-in-law of one of the conspirators, not to attend Parliament on November 5, Monteagle's suspicions were aroused. The government was alerted, the palace was searched, and Guy Fawkes was caught red-handed guarding the gunpowder. Carried to the Tower of London, Fawkes was mercilessly tortured until he gave the names of his fellow conspirators. Guy was executed in London's Old Palace Yard, Westminster in 1606.

    Today, Guy Fawkes Day is an important celebration in Britain. In the week before the holiday, children roam the streets

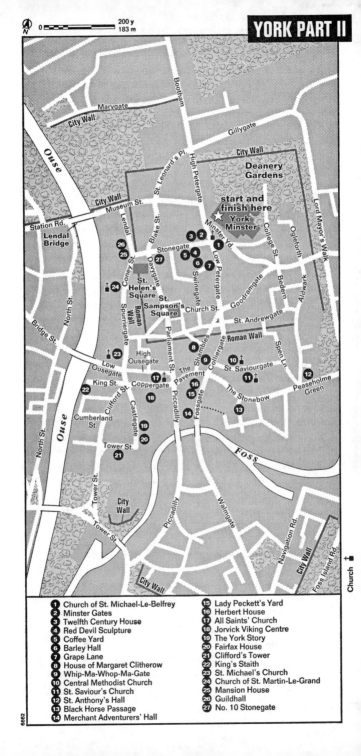

YORK PART II

0 ___ 200 y
0 ___ 183 m

Marygate

City Wall

Ouse

Bootham

Gillygate

City Wall

Deanery Gardens

St. Leonard's Pl.

High Petergate

Lord Mayor's Walk

City Wall

Museum St.

start and finish here
★ **York Minster**

Station Rd.

Lendal Bridge

Lendal

Blake St.

Minster Yd.

College St.

Ogleforth

❶

❸ ❷

Stonegate

❹

❺

❻ ❼

Low Petergate

Bedern

Aldwark

❷❻
❷❺

Coney St.

Davygate

❷❼

St. Helen's Square

Swinegate

St. Sampson's Square

❷❹

Roman Wall

Church St.

Goodramgate

St. Andrewgate

Roman Wall

Bridge St.

North St.

Spurriergate

Parliament St.

The Shambles

❽

❾

Collier gate

❿

St. Saviourgate

Spen Ln.

❶❶

Peaseholme Green

❶❷

High Ousegate

❷❸

Low Ousegate

King St.

❷❷

Coppergate

❶❼

❶❽

Clifford St.

The Pavement

Fossgate

❶❻

❶❺

The Stonebow

❶❸

Ouse

Cumberland St.

Castlegate

❶❹

Piccadilly

❶❾

❷❿

Tower St.

❷❶

Foss

Tower St.

City Wall

Piccadilly

Walmgate

Navigation Rd.

City Wall

City Wall

Tower St.

Foss Island Rd.

Church ✝

❶ Church of St. Michael-Le-Belfrey
❷ Minster Gates
❸ Twelfth Century House
❹ Red Devil Sculpture
❺ Coffee Yard
❻ Barley Hall
❼ Grape Lane
❽ House of Margaret Clitherow
❾ Whip-Ma-Whop-Ma-Gate
❿ Central Methodist Church
❶❶ St. Saviour's Church
❶❷ St. Anthony's Hall
❶❸ Black Horse Passage
❶❹ Merchant Adventurers' Hall

❶❺ Lady Peckett's Yard
❶❻ Herbert House
❶❼ All Saints' Church
❶❽ Jorvick Viking Centre
❶❾ The York Story
❷❿ Fairfax House
❷❶ Clifford's Tower
❷❷ King's Staith
❷❸ St. Michael's Church
❷❹ Church of St. Martin-Le-Grand
❷❺ Mansion House
❷❻ Guildhall
❷❼ No. 10 Stonegate

6662

carrying effigies of Guy Fawkes asking passersby for "a penny for the guy." The money goes toward building a bonfire, and on the night of November 5, countless bonfires, some house-size, are ignited across the nation to the traditional chant:

> *Remember, remember the 5th of November*
> *Gunpowder, treason and plot . . ."*

Exit the church of St. Michael-le-Belfrey, turn left onto Minster Yard, and left again onto High Petergate to:

REFUELING STOP **The Guy Fawkes Tavern,** 25 High Petergate (tel. 0904/671001). Believed to have been the birthplace of Guy Fawkes, on the 13th of April, 1570, the building is now a tavern where traditional English "pub grub" is served along with a good selection of ales and bitters.

Exit the tavern, turn right onto High Petergate, and walk about one block to:

2. Minster Gates, one of the main entrances to the Minster Library, intended for foot traffic only. There have been posts here for about 600 years. Originally, this approach was called "Bookland Lane." After the invention of printing, the route was known as "Bookbinders Alley." The statue you see here is of Minerva, the goddess of wisdom. Created by John Wolstenholme in 1801, the figure is leaning on a pile of books.

Turn right onto Stonegate, an ancient paved road that was once the main route for carrying stone to York Minster. This road has been in daily use for about 1,900 years. About one block ahead, turn right, into the narrow passage with "no. 52" on it. This leads to the ruins of:

3. Twelfth Century House, an A.D. 1180 construction that claims the title of York's oldest-surviving (barely) dwelling. Originally a two-story building, only a small portion of the top floor still remains. You can still see some 800-year-old decorative details.

Retrace your footsteps to Stonegate and turn right. Continue, noticing the sign that dominates the street—Ye Olde Starre Inn—York's oldest licensed inn, dating from 1644. One block before the Olde Starre, stop outside 33 Stonegate. On the left, by the entrance to Coffee Yard, you will see the:

4. **Red Devil Sculpture** that's chained to the wall about seven feet off the ground. "Devil" was the old term for young errand boys who were employed by the area's printers. Printers used to jestingly blame typesetting errors on these "mischievous" boys.
   Turn immediately left into:

5. **Coffee Yard,** a small lane that was home to York's earliest newspaper, the *York Mercury,* first printed on February 23, 1719. The yard was named by the Stonegate men who traded coffee here from the first half of the 17th century.

   A few doors down on your right is:

REFUELING STOP Thomas Gents Coffee House, 3 Coffee Yard (tel. 0904/647845). This restaurant and coffee shop is named for Thomas Gent, a printer in Coffee Yard who was best known for his newspapers *The Original York Journal* and *Weekly Courant.* When Gent moved from Stonegate to new premises in Petergate, his business declined. Gent died in 1778, in poverty at age 87.

An important feature of Georgian social life, coffeehouses were usually owned by women, but catered to an exclusively male clientele. Everyone is now allowed at Thomas Gents, where a visit seems to take you back to the year 1770. Pewter gleams above the fireplace, candles flicker in wall sconces, and 18th-century hats and wigs still hang on wall pegs. In addition to coffee, Thomas Gents offers a delicious selection of faithfully reproduced 18th-century English-style foods served by maids in period costume.

Exit Thomas Gents and turn left. The wooden building on your left is:

6. **Barley Hall,** Coffee Yard (tel. 0904/652398), a historical museum administered by the York Archaeological Trust. In the early 1480s Alderman Snawsell, a former lord mayor of York and wealthy goldsmith, rented this house from a nearby priory, and brought his family to live here. Now restored to its former splendor, Barley Hall is packed with rich medieval archives, and furnished in period style. Lavish hangings and fine furniture have been meticulously re-created. There is a small admission charge.

   Exit Barley Hall and turn left onto Coffee Yard, which ends at:

7. **Grape Lane,** a rather unimposing street that was known for prostitution in the 14th century. As was customary in medieval

times, English streets were named for activities that transpired therein. Since the street namers always called a spade a spade, this thoroughfare was originally known as "Grapcunt Lane"— *grap* was a bastardization of the word "grope."

Walk half a block on Grape Lane, turn right onto Swinegate. Half a block along, turn right onto Back Swinegate, then almost immediately turn left onto Finkle Street, which was once known as Mucky Peg Lane. At the end of Finkle Street, turn left onto St. Sampson's Square to:

REFUELING STOP The Roman Bath Public House, St. Sampson's Square (tel. 0904/620455). Inside the pub is a glass window, where patrons can look down at the remains of a Roman bath. These ancient remains were discovered in 1930 during a refurbishment of the pub. From here you can see a corner of the Roman *frigidarium* (cold bath), part of the *caldarium* (hot bath), and *hypocaust* pillars upon which a raised, heated floor rested.

Exit the pub and turn left, cross Church Street onto Silver Street, once the site of medieval York's silversmiths. After one block, turn left onto Newgate, then right into the market that begins opposite no. 12 Newgate. At the end of the first row of stalls, turn left onto the cobblestone walkway called Little Shambles, then turn right onto Shambles. One block ahead, on your right, is:

8. The House of Margaret Clitherow, 35 Shambles. After the reign of Roman Catholic Mary I ("Bloody Mary"), when Protestant Queen Elizabeth I held the throne, banned Catholic priests wandered the country holding services at great personal risk. Margaret Clitherow, who was born on this street in 1556 and married a local butcher at age 15, undertook the dangerous job of smuggling Catholic priests in and out of York. Caught in 1586, Clitherow was tried at the Assizes. She refused to plead guilty or not guilty in order to preserve her property, which would otherwise have been confiscated, and received the sentence prescribed for non-pleaders: death by pressing. She was placed under a heavy wooden door and rocks were piled on top until life was literally pressed from her body.

Continue to the end of Shambles and turn left onto the narrow, unnamed passageway just before the main road. Walk through the iron gates and turn right, onto York's shortest street, wonderfully named:

9. **Whip-Ma-Whop-Ma-Gate.** If you find this a mouth full, give thanks that the street isn't still known by its 16th-century name, "Whitnourwhatnourgate." Contrary to popular belief, the street's name has nothing to do with wife whipping. Rather, Whip-Ma-Whop-Ma-Gate is believed to be the medieval equivalent of "what kind of street do you call this."

Walk straight onto St. Saviourgate. One block ahead, on your left, is:

10. **The Central Methodist Church,** constructed in 1840 to mark the 100th anniversary of Methodism. It's built to accommodate 1,500 worshipers.

One block ahead, on St. Saviourgate, is:

11. **St. Saviour's Church,** a decommissioned church that dates from 1090, but was wholly rebuilt in 1844 and 1845. St. Saviour's is now the headquarters of York's Archaeological Resource Center (tel. 0904/613711). Open from February through November, the center can be visited to see many of the city's unearthed finds.

Continue walking along St. Saviourgate, turn right onto St. Saviour's Place, then left onto Peaseholme Green. About half a block on your left is:

12. **St. Anthony's Hall** the ancient meeting place of the Guild of St. Anthony, a religious organization established in 1418 to help its members get into heaven. Construction of this hall began around the year 1450. The guild was dissolved in 1627.

Diagonally across the road is:

REFUELING STOP The Black Swan Inn, Peaseholme Green (no phone). This delightful timber-framed medieval structure was once the home of William Bowes, a wealthy 15th-century merchant who was elected sheriff of York and then lord mayor in 1417 and 1428, respectively. Bowes represented York in London's Parliament during the reign of King Henry V. He was an ancestor of the Queen Mother.

In the 18th century, this building was home to the parents of General James Wolfe, the commander of the English forces that fought the French for Québec, Canada. At that time, a room on the second floor was used for the illegal sport of cock-fighting; a grille was built into the wall overlooking the house's stairs which enabled the gamblers to keep an eye out for unwelcome visitors.

The pub serves standard pub fare, along with the usual selection of beers.

Exit The Black Swan Inn and backtrack along Peaseholme Green into The Stonebow—a long, relatively uneventful walk past several car showrooms. Just past the telephone boxes, turn left into the dark and dingy:

13. Black Horse Passage. In Victorian times, this passage was used by gentlemen to make their way stealthily, under cover of darkness, to the city's nearby red-light district. The red brick wall on your right was built atop stones of an old Carmelite priory that once stood here. The missing stones—20,000 in total—were sold for £6 in 1358, to build the nearby Merchant Adventurers' Hall.

At the end of Black Horse Passage, turn right onto Straker's Passage, another delightfully seedy alleyway that captures the shady atmosphere of the district's less-than-innocent past. Turn left onto Fossgate, cross the street, and turn right through the red doors between no. 39 to 41 into:

14. Merchant Adventurers' Hall, Fossgate (tel. 0904/65-4818), the medieval guild of venture capitalists—those who risk their own money in trade. The guild's coat of arms, which sports the motto "May God Prosper Our Affairs" can be seen above the hall's front entrance.

The building's main room, the Great Hall, dates from 1357 to 1361 and is framed in timbers of English oak. It was in this room that most of northern England's medieval wealth was created. Here merchants conducted their business dealings in wool, woolens, and lead, and traded with London and many ports in Europe. The Merchant Adventurers brought back to York all manner of goods including lumber, wine, sugar, spices, dried fruits, dyes, drugs, furs, and silks.

The building's undercroft was used as a hospital in which 13 disadvantaged people (the number of Christ and the Twelve Apostles) were taken care of, free. The niches where patients kept their belongings can still be seen beside centuries-old scorch marks from illuminating torches.

The historical importance of Merchant Adventurers' Hall cannot be underestimated. In all of Europe, no other medieval guildhall survives with its business room, hospital, and chapel all intact and still owned by the same company that built it. The hall now contains an exhibition detailing the history of the merchants, highlighting their influence during the centuries in which York was, after London, the most important city in England. Admission is charged.

Exit Merchant Adventurers' Hall, turn left onto Fossgate, then left again, just past no. 47 Fossgate, into:

15. Lady Peckett's Yard. This street's name commemorates the wife of John Peckett, York's lord mayor from 1702 to 1703. According to custom, the wife of a lord mayor was called "Lady" for the rest of her life, even if her husband only served for a single year—an old verse reads: "He is a lord for a year and a day, but she is a lady forever and aye."

Walk to the far right side of this alley, where a passageway leads to Pavement, one of the city's first paved streets. The building immediately to your right is:

16. Herbert House, a 1620 construction that is widely celebrated as one of the finest timbered houses in York. Famed for its richly carved woodwork, the building was constructed without a basement, owing to the noticeable sag in the beam that supports the second floor. Christopher Herbert, a wealthy merchant and lord mayor of London, bought this plot of land in 1557 and set about building a typical large medieval town house. Herbert's son built the present structure, but his grandson, Sir Thomas Herbert, abandoned the property in 1649 after his close friend, King Charles I, was executed.

Turn left onto Pavement, and take the right fork onto High Ousegate. Immediately on your left is:

17. All Saints' Church, a 14th- and 15th-century building topped by a 19th-century lantern tower that is one of the landmarks of the York skyline, a reproduction of a medieval tower that used to shine a light to guide wayfarers to the city from the nearby forest of Galtres.

Enter the church, noticing the unusual door knocker. Dating from the 12th century, the knocker is known as a "doom," and depicts a beast swallowing a human. As was common in the Middle Ages, door knockers were a symbol of a church's protection for wrongdoers who, by entering the building, could claim sanctuary from pursuing government officials.

All Saints' had numerous connections with the city's local guilds, and the shields of many of them are displayed on the church's south wall. According to historical records, 46 lord mayors are buried inside this church.

Exit All Saints' Church, turn left onto High Ousegate, then immediately left again onto the pathway that leads to Coppergate. Cross Coppergate at the pedestrian crosswalk, and continue straight ahead into the pathway of Coppergate Shopping Precinct. Walk one block and turn right, into:

18. The Jorvick Viking Centre, a historical theme ride through ancient York. The Viking city, discovered below the ground level of the present street, has been reconstructed as it was in 948, and is a kind of high-tech museum; visitors ride in "time cars" through centuries of history. At the end of the ride is a display of artifacts. There is an admission charge.

Visit the Jorvick Viking Centre for an educational, if whimsical, rest, then continue walking along the Coppergate Shopping Precinct pathway. Turn right onto the alleyway that's just past St. Mary's Church, then walk straight to the entrance of:

19. The York Story, a museum and heritage center in St. Mary's Church, containing exhibits that trace the city's history over the last several hundred years. The decommissioned church in which this exhibition is housed dates from the 11th century, although there was a considerable amount of rebuilding in the 15th century. The church has the distinction of having the tallest spire in York at a height of 152 feet. There is an admission charge.

Exit The York Story, follow the alleyway to Castlegate, and turn left. About half a block ahead, on your left, is:

20. Fairfax House, Castlegate (tel. 0904/655543). Built in 1762 as a home for Viscount Fairfax, Fairfax House was created by a team of handpicked craftsmen specializing in woodwork, stonework, metalwork, and plasterwork, and remains as the finest example of Georgian architecture in York. Unfortunately, Viscount Fairfax died within 10 years of his home's completion. Over the next 200 years the house was used for a variety of functions, including a cinema and dance hall. Saved from near collapse by the York Civic Trust, Fairfax House was lovingly renovated to house one of England's best collections of mid-18th-century clocks and furniture. There is an admission charge.

Exit Fairfax House and continue walking along Castlegate. Turn right onto Tower Street and look left, at the structure on top of the hill. This is:

21. Clifford's Tower, one of the old battlements of York Castle. Erected by King Henry III, the tower replaces a wooden structure destroyed in a tragic event—it was burned down in 1190 in a mob attack on a group of Jews who had taken refuge there. The present 13th-century tower is named for Roger de Clifford, a leader of the house of Lancaster who was executed in 1322; his body hung in chains from this tower. Today, you can climb to the top of Clifford's Tower, an effort that rewards visitors with one of York's finest views.

Continue along Tower Street, turn right onto Clifford Street, then left onto Cumberland Street. Walk to the River Ouse and turn right onto:

22. King's Staith, a road associated with royal visits to York by kings Edward I, Edward II, and Edward III in the 13th and 14th centuries. The street was originally named "Pudding Holes," a term originating from the Old English word *pudd,* meaning "ditch." Ditches were dug along the riverbank where the public washed their meat and clothes. Because of this activity, a 15th-century law was passed prohibiting the dumping of waste into the river upstream from this point.

Walk two blocks along King's Staith to:

REFUELING STOP   The Kings Arms, King's Staith (tel. 0904/465-9435). The portrait and coat of arms on this inn's signs are of King Richard III, who visited the city after his coronation in 1483. Having come from York, the monarch was enthusiastically welcomed by the city's townsfolk. Richard reigned until 1485, when he was defeated and slain by Henry Tudor at the Battle of Bosworth.

According to historians, Richard is one of the most defamed personalities in English history. Shakespeare's portrait of the 15th-century king as a curled hunchback shuffling his way through a winter of discontent was long accepted, but it's probable that this mistaken profile of the monarch is the result of a successful propaganda campaign by Henry Tudor. Shakespeare was, of course, writing in an age when the slightest suggestion that questioned the legitimacy of the Tudors could be treasonable, and was, to say the least, unwise.

The Kings Arms is a delightful pub, but its riverside location means that it is prone to flooding. Inside the front door is a measuring pole marked with the various flood levels recorded over the years. On the pub's walls are photographs of various floodings, including one taken on February 25, 1991, showing the pub's owner being saved from an upstairs window by rescuers in a rowboat.

The pub serves lunch Monday through Friday, and is open from 11am to 11pm Monday through Saturday, noon to 3pm and 7pm to 10:30pm on Sunday.

Exit the pub, turn right up the stairs. At the top, turn right onto Low Ousegate. At the end of Low Ousegate, cross left over the pedestrian crossing and turn left onto Spurriergate to:

23. St. Michael's Church, a Norman-era church that was largely rebuilt in 1821. It's worth going inside to see the church's splendid Norman arcades.

Exit St. Michael's Church and continue walking along Spurriergate, which soon becomes Coney Street, York's main shopping thoroughfare. Originally known as *Cuningestrete,* from the Danish word *Kunung,* meaning "king." There has been a street here since Roman times. Walk five blocks along Coney Street to the 15th-century:

24. Church of St. Martin-le-Grand. Notice the clock on the church that overhangs Coney Street. It was erected in 1668 and refurbished in 1778. The little figure of an admiral on top of the clock is holding a sextant which, until it was damaged by German bombing in the 1940s, rotated.

Enter the church taking particular note of the Great West Window, one of England's finest 15th-century stained-glass windows. Removed for safekeeping before World War II, then refitted into the church's new north wall, the window depicts 13 scenes from the life of St. Martin of Tours. It was a gift to the church in 1437 from Vicar Robert Semer, whose likeness can be seen kneeling at the window's bottom.

Exit the Church of St. Martin-le-Grand and walk two more blocks along Coney Street to:

25. Mansion House, the official residence of York's lord mayor. Built from 1725 to 1730, the luxurious home was constructed to dissuade mayors from "retirement to the country during their term of office."

Continue walking along Coney Street and turn left, through the set of gates that lead to:

26. Guildhall, the main meeting and eating place for York's medieval crafts unions. The present building dates in part from 1446. A major part of the building, however, was destroyed during a German air strike on April 29, 1942. The restored hall is an exact replica of its predecessor, and is well worth a visit. Don't miss the modern stained-glass window which portrays the city's long and colorful history.

Exit Guildhall through the gates in which you entered and cross Coney Street directly into St. Helen's Square. Cross the Square onto Stonegate, and walk two blocks to:

27. No. 10 Stonegate, a fine black-and-white timbered building with a carving of a mermaid on its front. Probably a ship's figurehead, the mermaid statue recalls the days when York was a thriving port city. Many of the city's wooden buildings were constructed from timber culled from ships that were abandoned at York's riverside quays.

Continue walking to the end of Stonegate, turn left onto High Petergate and you will return to York Minster, the starting point of this tour.

Essentials

All of our walking tour destinations can be reached from London, either by car or by train or by bus—called "coach" in England (the term "bus" means a city bus).

BATH

Bath, about 110 miles west of London is a favorite excursion from the city. Bath (pop. 83,000) is situated along the River Avon, which is traversed by two bridges: North Parade Bridge and Pulteney Bridge. Most of the city's main sights are crowded around the bridgeheads and the centrally located abbey. Both the bus (tel. 0225/464446) and train (tel. 0225/463075) stations are located at the end of Manvers Street, within easy walking distance to the city center.

GETTING THERE

BY TRAIN BritRail trains depart from London's Paddington Station (tel. 071/262-6767) every 90 minutes and make the trip in about 80 minutes.

BY COACH National Express (tel. 071/730-0202) buses leave daily from London's Victoria Coach Station, and make the trip in about three hours.

BY CAR From London, take the M4 motorway to Exit 18.

CAMBRIDGE

Cambridge is only 55 miles north of London, easily reached by car or public transportation. There are two main thoroughfares in Cambridge (pop. 103,000). Trumpington Street, which becomes King's Parade, Trinity Street, and finally St. John's Street runs parallel to the River Cam, and is close to several of the city's colleges. The main shopping street starts at Magdalene Bridge, and turns into Bridge Street, Sidney Street, St Andrew's Street, and finally Regent Street.

GETTING THERE

BY TRAIN BritRail trains depart from London's Liverpool Street (tel. 071/283-7171) and King's Cross (tel. 071/278-2477) stations every 20 minutes and make the trek in about an hour. Once at Cambridge station, take the Cityrail bus link to Market Square, in the center of the city.

BY COACH National Express coaches (tel. 071/730-0202) depart from London's Victoria Coach Station 13 times each day. The ride to Cambridge takes an hour and 50 minutes.

BY CAR From London, take the M11 motorway to Exit 11.

CHESTER

Chester is about 207 miles northwest of London and lies 19 miles south of Liverpool. Most of the sightseeing is within the walled city; Eastgate is the main entrance.

GETTING THERE

BY TRAIN BritRail trains depart from London's Euston Station (tel. 071/387-7070), and make the trip in about 2 hours, 15 minutes. Because some trains are not direct and take much longer, it is wise to phone in advance for information. Chester can also be reached from Liverpool, a 45-minute trip, with trains departing every 30 minutes.

BY COACH National Express coaches depart from London's

Victoria Coach Station (tel. 071/730-0202). Journey time is 4 hours, 35 minutes. A National Express bus runs every hour between Birmingham and Chester, and there is service by the same line between Liverpool and Chester.

BY CAR From London head north on the M1, crossing onto the M6 at the junction. Continue northwest, and turn onto the M54. Near the end of the M54, pick up the A41 and travel northwest for the final lap of the journey.

OXFORD

Oxford is only 57 miles northwest of London, about an hour's trip. If you arrive by train, one of the city's new electric buses will take you to the town center free on presentation of your railway ticket. Both the train and bus stations are to the west of the city center.

Although Oxford is a sizeable industrial city, it is not hard to find your way around. Carfax, the city center, is surrounded by the colleges of Oxford, and intersected at right angles by Cornmarket Street, St. Aldate's Street, Queen Street, and High Street. Magdalen Bridge lies past the east end of High Street.

GETTING THERE

BY TRAIN BritRail trains depart from London's Paddington Station (tel. 071/262-6767), and make the trip to Oxford in about an hour.

BY COACH Oxford Tube and Oxford CityLink (tel. 0865/711312) run competing bus services, both departing from London's Grosvenor Gardens, near Victoria Station. The journey takes about 90 minutes. Between the two services, buses depart six times per hour, seven days per week.

BY CAR From London, take the M40 to the A40, to the A420 (or the A423, the scenic route via Windsor and Henley). Don't drive into Oxford's city center, however, as parking and traffic are horrific. Free "Park and Ride" car lots are located on the main approaches to the north, south, and west sides of the city. Transport buses from these parking lots depart every 8 to 10 minutes.

STRAFORD-UPON-AVON

Stratford is 91 miles northwest of London, and 41 miles northwest of Oxford. Stratford's simple layout—unchanged since the Middle Ages—makes it easy to find your way around and is an important component of its charm. There are just three streets running parallel to the river, and three other streets at right angles to it. A trip to Stratford can easily be combined with a trip to Oxford.

GETTING THERE

BY TRAIN The Shakespeare Connection rail/bus link departs from Euston Station, and takes about 2 hours. This is the only transport offering evening service back to London after the Stratford theaters close. Departures are Monday through Saturday at 9am, changing to the bus at Coventry and arriving at Stratford at 11:10am. Returns from Stratford are at 5:15pm or 11:15pm. Sunday departures are at 9:40am, returning at 5:55pm. BritRail trains also make the trip from London's Paddington Station (tel. 071/262-6767) with a change at Oxford, taking about 2½ hours.

BY COACH From Victoria Coach Station, the first National Express coach (tel. 071/730-0202) leaves at 10am, arriving in Stratford at approximately 1pm; the last coach leaves Stratford at 6:10pm.

BY CAR From London take the M40 motorway, then turn north on the A34.

YORK

York is 203 miles from London. The historical heart of the city is centered around York Minster, within the ancient city walls on either side of the River Ouse, which is crossed by three bridges, the Lendal, Ouse, and Skeldergate. The railroad station is near the city wall, on the west side of the old city.

GETTING THERE

BY PLANE British Midland flights arrive at the Leeds-Bradford Airport, a 50-minute flight from London's Heathrow Airport. Connecting buses at the airport take you east and the rest of the distance to York.

BY TRAIN From London's King's Cross Station (tel. 071/278-2477), trains leave for York every 10 minutes, a 2-hour trip.

BY COACH Four National Express coaches (tel. 071/730-0202) leave daily from London's Victoria Coach Station for York. The trip takes about 4½ hours.

BY CAR From London, head north on the M1 motorway. Cut northeast below Leeds at the junction of the A64 and head east to York.

FAST *ENGLAND'S CITIES*

Airports   For flight information for London airports, phone Heathrow Airport (tel. 081/759-4321), Gatwick Airport (tel. 0293/31299), or London City Airport (071/474-5555). Alternately, phone your airline directly.

American Express   American Express has offices in each of the city's covered in this guide: 99 St. Aldgate's, Oxford (tel. 0865/790099); 25 Sidney St., Cambridge (tel. 0223/351-636); 5 Bridge St., Bath (tel. 0225/444747); Bridgefoot, Stratford (tel. 0789/415856); 6 Stonegate, York (tel. 0904/670030); 23 St. Werburgh St., Chester (tel. 0244/431-1145). Most offices are open Monday through Friday from 9am to 6pm, Saturday from 9am to noon. To report lost or stolen cards, call London 071/222-9633, 24 hours.

Area Code   The telephone area code is 0865 in Oxford; 0223 in Cambridge; 0225 in Bath; 0789 in Stratford; 0904 in York; and 0244 in Chester. Area codes are necessary when dialing from outside the code.

Auto Rental   The big American car-rental firms are expensive, but most offer reduced rates for advance booking from the United States. Call for rates: **Avis** (tel. toll free 800/331-1084), **Hertz** (tel. toll free 800/654-3001).

If you wait until you reach London and rent from a local firm, expect to pay a higher cost per week depending on the season. The least expensive rentals I have found are from **Practical Used Car Rental,** 111 Bartholomew Rd., N.W. 5 (tel. 071/284-0199), and **Abbey Self Drive,** 10 York Way, N.1 (tel. 071/278-0118); Also look in the telephone directory under "Car Rental" for alternatives to the big American chains. Make sure that the rate you pay includes unlimited mileage, all taxes, and the collision-damage waiver, as these extras can send prices into the stratosphere.

Business Hours   Most banks are open Monday through Friday from 9:30am to 3:30pm. Some are also open Saturday from 9:30am to noon. Offices are generally open Monday through Friday from 8:30 or 9am until 5 or 5:30pm. Restaurants usually open for lunch at 11am, and stay open until 11pm or midnight. A very few stay open later. Stores are usually open Monday through Saturday from 10am to 6pm, but most stay open at least one extra hour one night during the week. By law, most stores are closed Sunday.

Currency   The English pound (£), a small, thick, round coin, is divided into 100 pence. Pence, abbreviated "p," come in 1p, 2p, 5p, 10p, and 50p coins. You may still see some 1- and 2-shilling coins, which are equivalent to 5p and 10p, respectively. Notes are issued in £5, £10, £20, and £50 denominations.

Currency Exchange   As a rule, you will get a better rate for traveler's checks than you will for cash. Banks generally offer the best exchange rates. Don't be afraid to use your credit cards; I've found that bank-card exchange rates not only are favorable but are regularly to my advantage when conversion costs are figured in.

Places with the longest hours (sometimes open all night) also offer the worst rates. Beware of *Chequepoint* and other high-commission bureaux de change.

Driving Rules   In Britain, wearing a seat belt is the law. You may not turn right on a red light, and automobiles must stop whenever a pedestrian steps into a crosswalk. Many crosswalks are located in the middle of the block, not at the corner. They are usually marked by white stripes on the pavement (zebra striping), and flashing orange lights on either sidewalk.

Drugstores   Pharmacies take turns staying open late. Phone the operator (100) and ask for the police for the opening hours and addresses of late-opening "chemists."

Electricity   English appliances operate on 220 volts and plug into three-pronged outlets that differ from those in America and on the Continent. Hairdryers, irons, shavers, and other electric goods designed for the American market must be equipped with an adapter and a transformer. Do not attempt to plug an American appliance into a European electrical outlet without a transformer; you will ruin you appliance and possibly start a fire.

Embassies   The U.S. Embassy, 24 Grosvenor Sq., London W.1 (tel. 071/499-9000), does not accept visitors—all inquiries must be made by mail or phone. The Canadian High Commission is in Australia House on the Strand, London W.C.2 (tel. 071/379-4334), and is open Monday through Friday from 9am to 1pm. The New Zealand High Commission is in New Zealand House, Haymarket, London S.W.1 (tel. 071/930-8422), open Monday through Friday from 9am to 5pm.

Emergencies   Police, fire, and ambulance can be reached by dialing 999 from any phone. No money is required.

Information   Bath's Tourist Information Centre is in the Colonades Shopping Centre, Bath Street (tel. 0225/462831), opposite the Roman Baths, open May through October, Monday through Saturday from 9:30am to 8pm, Sunday from 10am to 6pm; November through April, Monday through Saturday from 9:30am to 5pm, Sunday from 10am to 4pm.

The Cambridge Tourist Information Centre is at Wheeler Street (tel. 0223/322640) behind the Guildhall.

The Chester Tourist Information Centre is at the Town Hall, Northgate Street (tel. 0244/313126).

The Oxford Information Centre, St. Aldate's Chambers, St. Aldate's (tel. 0865/726871), can provide you with maps, brochures, and other information, and is open Monday through Saturday from 9:30am to 5pm, Sunday from 10am to 3:30pm.

Stratford-upon-Avon's Tourist Information Centre, Bridgefoot (tel. 0789/293127), is open March through October, Monday through Saturday from 9am to 5:30pm, Sunday from 2 to 5pm; November through February, Monday through Saturday from 10:30am to 4pm.

York's Tourist Information Centre is at De Grey Rooms, Exhibition Square (tel. 0904/621756).

Liquor Laws   Under British law, no one under 18 years of age may legally purchase or consume alcohol. Beer and wine are sold by supermarkets, liquor stores (called "bottle shops"), and food shops advertising "off-license" sales. Some supermarkets also sell stronger spirits, at some of the best prices in town.

Lost Property   To report a loss or theft, call the operator (100) and ask for the police. They will direct you to the appropriate lost-and-found office.

Mail   Post offices are plentiful and are normally open Monday through Friday from 9am to 5pm, Saturday from 9am to noon. Mailboxes, which are round and red, are well distributed throughout each of the cities covered in this guidebook.

You can receive mail in London, marked "Post Restante," and addressed to you, care of the London Chief Post Office, King Edward Street, London EC1A 1AA, England. The office is located near St. Paul's Cathedral and is open Monday through Friday from 8:30am to 6:30pm. You will need to show identification to collect your mail. If you have an American Express card, or are carrying traveler's checks issued by that company, you can receive mail care of any American Express office (see above).

Newspapers and Magazines   The extraordinarily large number of newspapers in England are generally divided into two categories—broadsheets and tabloids. In general, tabloids like *The Sun, Today,* and *Daily Mirror* sensationalize news more than the larger-format papers. *The Times* is the grandaddy of England's opinionated papers, and features a particularly hefty Sunday edition. The *Guardian* is the country's largest left-of-center paper, with in-depth investigative stories and good local reporting. The *Daily Telegraph,* known in some circles as the "Torygraph," leans to the right politically, and is particularly strong in foreign coverage. The *Independent,* one of the country's newest newspapers, is trying to make inroads with solid middle-of-the-road reporting. This paper features Britain's best arts section every Sunday.

Police   In an emergency, dial 999 from any phone; no money is needed. At other times, dial the operator (100) and ask to be connected with the police.

Restrooms   Even if you don't drink, you'll find England's many pubs handy for their facilities. My first pick for restrooms, however, is the lobby-level lavatories in the city's better-known hotels.

Safety   Whenever you're traveling in an unfamiliar city or country, stay alert. Be aware of your immediate surroundings. Wear a moneybelt and keep a close eye on your possessions. Be particularly careful with cameras, purses, and wallets, all favorite targets for thieves and pickpockets.

Taxes   Unlike in the United States, where tax is tacked on at the register, England has a 17.5% value-added tax (VAT). It is often included in menu prices, though sometimes it is added to the bill, along with a service charge; the policy is usually written on the menu. There is no additional airport tax upon departure, and tax is included in all hotel rates. Foreign tourists can reclaim the VAT for major purchases.

Telephone   Two kinds of pay phones are regularly used. One accepts coins and the other uses a phonecard, available from newsagents. Phonecard telephones automatically deduct the price of your call from the card. Cards are especially handy if you want to call abroad, as you don't have to continuously pop in the pounds. Some large hotels and touristy street corners also have credit-card telephones that accept major credit cards. Lift the handle and follow the instructions on the screen.

To reach the local operator, dial 100. The international operator is 155. Information (called "directory inquiries") can be reached by dialing 142 and is free of charge.

Television   The BBC produces some great television programs, but they're few and far between. There are only four English television stations, so you can quickly flip through the channels before deciding there's nothing on. Many hotels now offer stations from the European Cable Network. These include Eurosport, a sports channel; Sky News, a 24-hour news channel; and MTV, a clone of the American version.

Time   England's clocks are set on Greenwich mean time, five hours ahead of U.S. eastern standard time. Clocks here spring forward and fall back for daylight saving time, but the semiannual ritual commences on a slightly different schedule than in the States. To find out the exact time by phone, dial Timeline (tel. 123).

Tipping   Most restaurants automatically add a service charge. The restaurant's policy will be written on the menu. When a service charge is not included, a 10% to 15% tip is customary. Taxi drivers expect 10% to 15% of the fare. Note that tipping is rare in both pubs and theaters.

Tourist Information   See "Information," above.

Water   There's plenty of it here and, compared to many capital cities, it's relatively safe to drink. Designer waters like Perrier are popular at restaurants; specify tap water if that's what you want.

Weather   Weathercall (tel. 0898/500401) keeps tabs on the temperature and readies you for the next rainfall.

RECOMMENDED READING

Before starting your walks in our favorite English cities, you may wish to read something about them. Those who prefer inspiration in the form of novels and poetry will not be disappointed since each of our cities has played a prominent role in England's literary history. All the works mentioned below appear (unless noted) in Viking Penguin paperback editions and are available from most large chain bookstores.

The colleges of Cambridge once housed such writers as Edmund Spenser, John Milton, William Wordsworth, Lord Byron, E.M. Forster, and A.A. Milne (author of the "Winnie-the-Pooh" books). You may wish to check out Wordsworth's *Prelude* or Byron's *Juvenilia* for references to Cambridge as well as Milton's Cambridge poems. For those who prefer novels, E.M. Forster's *Maurice* (W.W. Norton, 1993) is set in part in "Sunington," a stand-in for Cambridge.

Oxford, too, has a strong literary heritage in J.R.R. Tolkien, C.S. Lewis, and Oscar Wilde. It has been portrayed in such novels as Thomas Hardy's *Jude the Obscure* (as "Chrisminster"), where Jude toils as a stonemason but never is able to attend classes; in Evelyn Waugh's *Brideshead Revisited* (Little, Brown, 1982), where Charles Ryder first encounters Sebastian Flyte; and most recently in William Nicholson's bittersweet play and film *Shadowlands* (NAL/Plume, 1991), which portrays the courtship and marriage of C.S. Lewis and the American Joy Gresham.

Bath has also proven to be a popular literary setting. Jane Austen, who visited Bath frequently on holiday as a young woman, used it as a setting in two of her novels. In *Northanger Abbey* the young heroine Catherine Morland is taken to Bath by her friends Mr. and Mrs. Allan where she meets Henry Tilney, and a good portion of *Persuasion* also takes place in Bath. Bath is a major destination in both Charles Dickens's *The Pickwick Papers* and Tobias Smollett's eighteenth-century epistolary novel *Humphrey Clinker*.

York and Chester are well represented by two of the four surviving complete cycles of mystery, or miracle plays. Performed throughout the Middle Ages on the feast day of Corpus Christi by members of the local guilds, these plays reenacted the stories of the Bible, from Genesis to Revelation; appropriately, York's shipwrights usually presented the story of Noah. If you would like to read further about mystery plays, a good place to start is with Peter Happés *The English Mystery Plays,* which includes examples from both the York and Chester cycles.

Stratford-upon-Avon's literary fame is of a more singular nature and also quite well known.

If you prefer your background reading to be more strictly factual, we offer a bibliography of non-fiction titles on our six favorite cities. The list below includes some of the better books on history and culture in our six cities. We've listed paperback editions widely available in the United States whenever possible.

Ackroyd, Peter. *Dickens* (HarperCollins, 1992–pap.).

Basildon, Dacre. *Oxford Life* (Eyre and Spottiswoode).

Carlton, Charles. *Charles I: The Personal Monarch* (Routledge Chapman & Hall, 1984—pap.).

Carpenter, Humphrey. *Tolkien: A Biography* (Houghton Mifflin, 1988—pap.).

Carpenter, Humphrey. *W. H. Auden: A Biography* (Houghton Mifflin, 1982—pap.).

Chainey, Graham. *A Literary History of Cambridge* (University of Michigan Press, 1986—pap.).

Cheetham, Hal. *Portrait of Oxford* (Robert Hale, 1971).

Clarke, Anne. *Lewis Carroll: A Biography* (J.M. Dent & Sons Ltd., 1979).

Defoe, Daniel. *Tour Through the Whole Island of Great Britain* (Viking Penguin, 1988—pap.).

Delaney, Frank. *Betjeman Country* (Hodder and Stoughton/John Murray, 1983).

Doherty, Francis M. *Byron* (Evans Brothers Ltd., 1968).

Eagle, Dorothy, and Hilary Carnell (eds.). *The Oxford Illustrated Literary Guide to Great Britain and Ireland,* 2nd ed. (Oxford University Press, 1992).

Ellman, Richard. *Oscar Wilde* (Random House, 1988—pap.)

Fido, Martin. *Oscar Wilde: The Dramatic Life and Fascinating Times of Oscar Wilde* (The Hamlyn Publishing Group, 1973).

Fowler, Laurence, and Helen. *Cambridge Commemorated: An Anthology of University Life* (Cambridge University Press, 1984).

Hayman, Ronald. *My Cambridge* (Parkwest Publications, 1987—pap.).

Hibbert, Christopher, and Anthony Hibbert. *The Encyclopedia of Oxford* (Macmillan).

Horridge, Glenn K., and John Janaway. *Cambridge: A Short History* (Ammonite Books, 1987).

Irving, Washington. *Notes & Journal of Travel in Europe* (Scholarly Press).

James, Henry. *Portraits of Places* (Reprint of 1883 ed.; Ayer Co.).

Jones, Mark. *Snickelways of York* (Maxiprint, 1983).

Kay, Dennis. *Shakespeare: His Life Work and Era* (William Morrow, 1994—pap.).

Lane, Maggie. *A Charming Place: Bath in the Life and Novels of Jane Austen* (Millstream Books, 1988).

Levin, Robert E. *Bill Clinton: The Inside Story* (S.P.I. Books, 1992).

Look Up in Cambridge (Gemma Books, 1985).

Lowndes, William. *They Came to Bath* (Radcliffe Press Ltd., 1982).

Matthews, Rupert. *Haunted York* (Pitkin).

Morris, Jan. *Oxford*, 3rd ed. (Oxford University Press, 1988—pap.).

Morriss, Richard, and Ken Hoverd. *The Buildings of Bath* (Alan Sutton Publishing Inc., 1983).

Pearson, Hesketh. *A Life of Shakespeare* (Hamish Hamilton, 1947; reprinted 1987—pap.).

Pepys, Samuel. *The Illustrated Pepys: Extracts from the Diary.* Edited by Robert Latham (University of California Press, 1978—pap.).
  The entire diary—unabridged—is also available in a library edition from University of California Press and can probably be found in a local university library.

Pile, Stephen. *The Book of Heroic Failures* (Ballantine, 1986—pap.).

Pudney, John. *Lewis Carroll and His World* (Scribner, 1976—pap.).

Reeve, Frank A. *The Cambridge Nobody Knows* (Oleander Press, 1977—pap.).

Rothnie, Niall. *Unknown Bath: Scandals and Secrets from the Past* (Ashgrove Press Ltd, 1986).

Schoenbaum, S. *William Shakespeare: A Compact Documentary Life* (Oxford University Press, 1987—pap.).

Smalley, Stephen S., the very Reverend. *Chester Cathedral* (English Life Publications, 1989).

Stanley, Louis I *The Cambridge Year* (Robert Hale, 1978)

Sugden, Marian. *Chester* (The Pevensey Press, 1986).

Weisz, Roland, and Russell P. O. Beach (eds.). *York Town and City Guide* (The Automobile Associate, 1987).

Whiteman, Yvonne. *The New Bath Guide* (Ashgrove Press Ltd., 1989).

Wilson, Jeremy. *Lawrence of Arabia: The Authorised Biography of T. E. Lawrence* (Macmillan, 1992—pap.).

Index

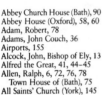

Please Send Me the Books Checked Below:

FROMMER'S COMPREHENSIVE GUIDES
(Guides listing facilities from budget to deluxe, with emphasis on the medium-priced)

	Retail Price	Code		Retail Price	Code
☐ Acapulco/Ixtapa/Taxco 1993–94	$15.00	C120	☐ Morocco 1992–93	$18.00	C021
☐ Alaska 1994–95	$17.00	C131	☐ Nepal 1994–95	$18.00	C126
☐ Arizona 1993–94	$18.00	C101	☐ New England 1994 (Avail. 1/94)	$16.00	C137
☐ Australia 1992–93	$18.00	C002	☐ New Mexico 1993–94	$15.00	C117
☐ Austria 1993–94	$19.00	C119	☐ New York State 1994–95	$19.00	C133
☐ Bahamas 1994–95	$17.00	C121	☐ Northwest 1994–95 (Avail. 2/94)	$17.00	C140
☐ Belgium/Holland/Luxembourg 1993–94	$18.00	C106	☐ Portugal 1994–95 (Avail. 2/94)	$17.00	C141
☐ Bermuda 1994–95	$15.00	C122	☐ Puerto Rico 1993–94	$15.00	C103
☐ Brazil 1993–94	$20.00	C111	☐ Puerto Vallarta/Manzanillo/Guadalajara 1994–95 (Avail. 1/94)	$14.00	C028
☐ California 1994–95	$15.00	C134	☐ Scandinavia 1993–94	$19.00	C135
☐ Canada 1994–95 (Avail. 4/94)	$19.00	C145	☐ Scotland 1994–95 (Avail. 4/94)	$17.00	C146
☐ Caribbean 1994	$18.00	C123	☐ South Pacific 1994–95 (Avail. 1/94)	$20.00	C138
☐ Carolinas/Georgia 1994–95	$17.00	C128	☐ Spain 1993–94	$19.00	C115
☐ Colorado 1994–95 (Avail. 3/94)	$16.00	C143	☐ Switzerland/Liechtenstein 1994–95 (Avail. 1/94)	$19.00	C139
☐ Cruises 1993–94	$19.00	C107	☐ Thailand 1992–93	$20.00	C033
☐ Delaware/Maryland 1994–95 (Avail. 1/94)	$15.00	C136	☐ U.S.A. 1993–94	$19.00	C116
☐ England 1994	$18.00	C129	☐ Virgin Islands 1994–95	$13.00	C127
☐ Florida 1994	$18.00	C124	☐ Virginia 1994–95 (Avail. 2/94)	$14.00	C142
☐ France 1994–95	$20.00	C132	☐ Yucatán 1993–94	$18.00	C110
☐ Germany 1994	$19.00	C125			
☐ Italy 1994	$19.00	C130			
☐ Jamaica/Barbados 1993–94	$15.00	C105			
☐ Japan 1994–95 (Avail. 3/94)	$19.00	C144			

FROMMER'S $-A-DAY GUIDES
(Guides to low-cost tourist accommodations and facilities)

	Retail Price	Code		Retail Price	Code
☐ Australia on $45 1993–94	$18.00	D102	☐ Israel on $45 1993–94	$18.00	D101
☐ Costa Rica/Guatemala/Belize on $35 1993–94	$17.00	D108	☐ Mexico on $45 1994	$19.00	D116
☐ Eastern Europe on $30 1993–94	$18.00	D110	☐ New York on $70 1994–95	$16.00	D120
☐ England on $60 1994	$18.00	D112	☐ New Zealand on $45 1993–94	$18.00	D103
☐ Europe on $50 1994	$19.00	D115	☐ Scotland/Wales on $50 1992–93	$18.00	D019
☐ Greece on $45 1993–94	$19.00	D100	☐ South America on $40 1993–94	$19.00	D109
☐ Hawaii on $75 1994	$19.00	D113	☐ Turkey on $40 1992–93	$22.00	D023
☐ India on $40 1992–93	$20.00	D010	☐ Washington, D.C. on $40 1994–95 (Avail. 2/94)	$17.00	D119
☐ Ireland on $45 1994–95 (Avail. 1/94)	$17.00	D117			

FROMMER'S CITY $-A-DAY GUIDES
(Pocket-size guides to low-cost tourist accommodations and facilities)

	Retail Price	Code		Retail Price	Code
☐ Berlin on $40 1994–95	$12.00	D111	☐ Madrid on $50 1994–95 (Avail. 1/94)	$13.00	D118
☐ Copenhagen on $50 1992–93	$12.00	D003	☐ Paris on $50 1994–95	$12.00	D117
☐ London on $45 1994–95	$12.00	D114	☐ Stockholm on $50 1992–93	$13.00	D022

FROMMER'S WALKING TOURS
(With routes and detailed maps, these companion guides point out the places and pleasures that make a city unique)

	Retail Price	Code		Retail Price	Code
☐ Berlin	$12.00	W100	☐ Paris	$12.00	W103
☐ London	$12.00	W101	☐ San Francisco	$12.00	W104
☐ New York	$12.00	W102	☐ Washington, D.C.	$12.00	W105

FROMMER'S TOURING GUIDES
(Color-illustrated guides that include walking tours, cultural and historic sights, and practical information)

	Retail Price	Code		Retail Price	Code
☐ Amsterdam	$11.00	T001	☐ New York	$11.00	T008
☐ Barcelona	$14.00	T015	☐ Rome	$11.00	T010
☐ Brazil	$11.00	T003	☐ Scotland	$10.00	T011
☐ Florence	$ 9.00	T005	☐ Sicily	$15.00	T017
☐ Hong Kong/Singapore/			☐ Tokyo	$15.00	T016
Macau	$11.00	T006	☐ Turkey	$11.00	T013
☐ Kenya	$14.00	T018	☐ Venice	$ 9.00	T014
☐ London	$13.00	T007			

FROMMER'S FAMILY GUIDES

	Retail Price	Code		Retail Price	Code
☐ California with Kids	$18.00	F100	☐ San Francisco with Kids (Avail. 4/94)	$17.00	F104
☐ Los Angeles with Kids (Avail. 4/94)	$17.00	F103	☐ Washington, D.C. with Kids (Avail. 2/94)	$17.00	F102
☐ New York City with Kids (Avail. 2/94)	$18.00	F101			

FROMMER'S CITY GUIDES
(Pocket-size guides to sightseeing and tourist accommodations and facilities in all price ranges)

	Retail Price	Code		Retail Price	Code
☐ Amsterdam 1993–94	$13.00	S110	☐ Montréal/Québec City 1993–94	$13.00	S125
☐ Athens 1993–94	$13.00	S114	☐ Nashville/Memphis 1994–95 (Avail. 4/94)	$13.00	S141
☐ Atlanta 1993–94	$13.00	S112	☐ New Orleans 1993–94	$13.00	S103
☐ Atlantic City/Cape May 1993–94	$13.00	S130	☐ New York 1994 (Avail. 1/94)	$13.00	S138
☐ Bangkok 1992–93	$13.00	S005	☐ Orlando 1994	$13.00	S135
☐ Barcelona/Majorca/Minorca/Ibiza 1993–94	$13.00	S115	☐ Paris 1993–94	$13.00	S109
☐ Berlin 1993–94	$13.00	S116	☐ Philadelphia 1993–94	$13.00	S113
☐ Boston 1993–94	$13.00	S117	☐ San Diego 1993–94	$13.00	S107
☐ Budapest 1994–95 (Avail. 2/94)	$13.00	S139	☐ San Francisco 1994	$13.00	S133
☐ Chicago 1993–94	$13.00	S122	☐ Santa Fe/Taos/Albuquerque 1993–94	$13.00	S108
☐ Denver/Boulder/Colorado Springs 1993–94	$13.00	S131	☐ Seattle/Portland 1994–95	$13.00	S137
☐ Dublin 1993–94	$13.00	S128	☐ St. Louis/Kansas City 1993–94	$13.00	S127
☐ Hong Kong 1994–95 (Avail. 4/94)	$13.00	S140	☐ Sydney 1993–94	$13.00	S129
☐ Honolulu/Oahu 1994	$13.00	S134	☐ Tampa/St. Petersburg 1993–94	$13.00	S105
☐ Las Vegas 1993–94	$13.00	S121	☐ Tokyo 1992–93	$13.00	S039
☐ London 1994	$13.00	S132	☐ Toronto 1993–94	$13.00	S126
☐ Los Angeles 1993–94	$13.00	S123	☐ Vancouver/Victoria 1994–95 (Avail. 1/94)	$13.00	S142
☐ Madrid/Costa del Sol 1993–94	$13.00	S124	☐ Washington, D.C. 1994 (Avail. 1/94)	$13.00	S136
☐ Miami 1993–94	$13.00	S118			
☐ Minneapolis/St. Paul 1993–94	$13.00	S119			

SPECIAL EDITIONS

	Retail Price	Code		Retail Price	Code
☐ Bed & Breakfast Southwest	$16.00	P100	☐ Caribbean Hideaways	$16.00	P103
☐ Bed & Breakfast Great American Cities (Avail. 1/94)	$16.00	P104	☐ National Park Guide 1994 (Avail. 3/94)	$16.00	P105
			☐ Where to Stay U.S.A.	$15.00	P102

Please note: if the availability of a book is several months away, we may have back issues of guides to that particular destination. Call customer service at (815) 734-1104.